Computing in
Linguistics and Ph

COMPUTING IN LINGUISTICS AND PHONETICS
Introductory Readings

edited by

Peter Roach
Department of Psychology
University of Leeds
Leeds

ACADEMIC PRESS

Harcourt Brace Jovanovich
London San Diego New York
Boston Sydney Tokyo Toronto

ACADEMIC PRESS LIMITED
24-28 Oval Road
London NW1 7DX

United States Edition published by
ACADEMIC PRESS INC.
San Diego, CA 92101

A catalogue record for this book is available from the British Library
ISBN 0-12-589340-X

Printed in Great Britain by T.J. Press (Padstow) Ltd, Padstow, Cornwall

Contents

Introduction

When you look around a department in a university or college where linguistics and phonetics are taught you are likely to see computers in widespread use, and you may wonder what the computers are used for. The purpose of this book is to introduce you to some of the many different ways in which this technology has become an important part of the subject. Many of those who work in our field (including those of us who have written this book) look on the introduction of the computer as one of the most interesting and important developments of recent decades.

In some cases, the use we make of computers is simple and obvious: for example, we all use them for word-processing, where the machine is used as a tool rather like a typewriter. If we lost our word-processors, we could still carry on our work, though the results would look much less smart and would probably take longer to produce. But there are now many areas of linguistics and phonetics in which work would come to a standstill without computers: in speech research, for example, high-quality speech synthesis requires computer control, while in linguistics, subjects such as machine translation and automatic parsing are completely dependent on these machines.

In each of the following chapters, the authors try to explain the use of computers in their own work or in a field which interests them. We do not claim to cover the whole field of computational linguistics and phonetics, though our interests are wide. An important objective of the book is to explain why we encourage our students to learn computing as part of their studies. Courses in computing are widely available, but this seems to be one of those subjects where the ideas are difficult to grasp if you cannot see how they relate to your own area of study, and students are often discouraged by trying to follow general-purpose computing courses taught by computer specialists. We believe that it is much better to learn through finding out how to use computers in your own chosen subject.

This book certainly does not aim to teach you how to use a computer, but it does set out to convince you that if you are studying linguistics, phonetics or some related discipline, computing is both relevant and rewarding as a subject to study.

As a final word of encouragement, we would like to point out that much of what we do with computers requires very little in the way of mathematical knowledge or scientific training. The most important attributes for successful learning of computing are the ability to think clearly and the willingness to experiment, and we find these in students from all kinds of academic backgrounds.

Acknowledgements

When we began work on this book, all of us were members of the Department of Linguistics and Phonetics at Leeds University. Now, many of us have moved on to other departments, other universities or other jobs, but we have all benefited from working with each other and with many other researchers and students who worked there with us. We would like to thank particularly Ted Allwood, Eric Castelli, Gustav Clark, Andrea Dew, Nancy Glaister, Esther Grabe, Hélène Knight, Helen Roach, Paul Rowlands and David Tugwell. All of us have depended on Eric Brearley, the department's chief technician, who has always coped cheerfully with the never-ending jobs thrown up by our computing requirements. None of us could have achieved what we have without the wisdom and patience of Robin Haigh, our former computing officer. We cannot remember a computing problem that he could not put right for us. We would also like to thank Dr. Mike MacMahon of Glasgow University, who read the manuscript and made many helpful suggestions for improvements, and Des O'Hara of the Graphics Department of Leeds University's Audio-Visual Service for his help with our diagrams.

If any readers of this book eventually work in computer-based research, we hope that they will be lucky enough to work, as we have, in a community where people help each other through the inevitable technical problems and make time to talk to each other.

1 Fundamental Concepts

PETER ROACH

As the Introduction said, this book does not aim to teach you how to use computers. However, in order for you to be able to understand what is being explained in some of the later chapters it is necessary to introduce some concepts and terminology that are used in practically all computing work. If you are already reasonably familiar with computers you will find that you do not need to read this chapter, but complete beginners should start here.

First, the computer itself. Most students start on small, individual machines that we call *microcomputers* or just *micros*. The best known of these in British educational establishments has for quite a few years been the BBC Micro, but this is gradually being replaced by more modern machines. Among other popular micros are the Apple Macintosh and the very large range of machines all based on the IBM PC design (these are usually just called PCs). There is also a PC-like micro specially designed for educational use called the RM Nimbus. An alternative way of learning computing (less popular these days than it was) is to have a big computer serving a whole group of users; each user has a *terminal* to communicate with the central machine, usually called the *mainframe*.

Perhaps the best arrangement of all is to provide students with micros that are capable of working as small independent computers but also, when required, as terminals connected to a more powerful computer. This sort of machine is often called a *workstation*. Connecting computers so that they can communicate with each other has become important for getting the most out of the equipment; it is known as *networking*.

The computers themselves, and all the various pieces of equipment that go with them, such as printers, are usually referred to as *hardware* when they need to be distinguished from the other main type of computing equipment: computer *software*. Software is the name for the *programs* that will be used on the computer for which they are provided (incidentally, it is usual to use the

American spelling for 'program' in this meaning). To give a very simple analogy, if you buy a piano you get a large wooden box containing mechanical components, but this hardware is quite distinct from the actual music that you play on it. Essentially a program is a set of written instructions that tell the computer what it must do, rather as the notes printed on sheet music tell the musician what notes to play and in what order.

Computer software can be divided into three main types: (1) operating systems, (2) packages and (3) languages.

(1) A comparatively simple electronic device like a digital watch or calculator is usually dedicated to doing just one job, but a computer has to be capable of doing hundreds of highly complex tasks without being told by the user how it should organise them; computer engineers have developed very sophisticated programs for managing computers, and these are known as *operating systems*. On some machines these are so unobtrusive that you hardly notice that they exist, while others (a good example is UNIX) take quite a long time to learn – usually because they are so complex and powerful.

(2) For many of the things that we want to do with computers, the programs we need already exist. If I want to do some statistics, for example, I could in theory write my own program to calculate all the figures that I need. This would be a waste of time, however, because I can use one of the many sets of programs that have been written by professionals to do the same calculations. These collections of programs are known as *packages*, and in general it is much easier to learn to use a package than to write your own programs; in addition, they usually work better than anything an amateur could produce. Other examples of packages are those for word-processing, graphics (that is, illustrations and diagrams) and the analysis of speech or of texts.

(3) There are times when you want to do something with a computer that cannot be done with existing packages. This situation usually arises in the context of postgraduate research, but it is often felt that learning to write programs is a good way of learning computing; many students are therefore taught how to do this even though it is unlikely that more than a few of them will have a genuine need to write programs in the foreseeable future. Programming is certainly an interesting intellectual exercise, and one that can change some of your ideas about human language; people used to say the same sort of thing in favour of learning Latin, of course.

When you write a program or use a package, the instructions you give the computer must be written in exactly the right way, with no ambiguities. Outside the world of computing we find similar situations where instructions have to be given to people in a way that leaves no room for mistakes, for example in cookery recipes, in aircraft maintenance manuals or in architects' plans. Each type of instruction-writing has its own set of conventions that users have to learn, and the same is true in computing. Probably the most important part of writing a program is to work out the general plan for how the various parts are to work and fit together; the general design (as opposed to the specific program code) is called an *algorithm*.

Each particular way of writing and putting together the instructions in a program is called a *language*, and there are many different computer languages available, each of which is good for certain purposes and less good for others. Most regular users of computers find that it is not very difficult to learn other computer languages – some say that it is like learning to drive a car that is different from the one you learned in. Computer specialists tend to hold very strong views about different languages, and to get passionately attached to their favourites.

Although the technical details of how computers work and how they differ from each other are not relevant here, there is something that does have important consequences, and this is the form in which a computer stores and retrieves its information. This is important because most people working in our field have to deal with large amounts of data and to share their data with each other – we use large amounts of linguistic and phonetic data in the hope that it will give a representative coverage of the language or style being studied. Computers can store a great deal of information in their own internal memory and disk storage, but for really large amounts (for example, a million words of English text, or half an hour of digitally recorded speech) and for moving data from place to place, the storage must be on some external device attached to the computer. Moderate amounts of data can be stored and transported on *floppy disks* – around a million letters of text, for example. Larger amounts have, until recently, been stored on large reels of magnetic tape or on tape cartridges like audio cassettes. The latest technique is to store data on a compact disk – usually the same type of disk as the musical ones you are familiar with. When we use this technology for storing computer data, it is known as *CD-ROM*. A large collection of linguistic material (for example, the complete works of Shakespeare, or all the issues of *The Times*) is called a *corpus*, while a more organised collection of information (e.g. a telephone directory or an encyclopedia stored on a computer) is known as a *database*.

Many people look on computing as an essentially numerical activity, but much of our work shows that this is not the case: a lot of what we do is non-mathematical, involving the manipulation of letters, words and sentences. Sequences of letters are called *strings*, and the bits of program that we use to analyse these strings are called *string functions*. It is usual to make a distinction between *word-processing* (which is the name we usually give to the use of a computer to do typing or document production) and *text-processing*, which is the scientific analysis of texts by computer.

You may find, when you start using a computer, that the keyboard looks dauntingly complicated. It is true that many special symbols are used in computing, but you are not likely to need many as a beginner, and you will learn how to use the others later. All keyboards have a main group of keys for the letters; many have a separate group of number keys laid out like a calculator keyboard – it is often much quicker to use these for typing in numerical data than to use the alternative number keys that are usually found at the top of the letters section. There are usually *function keys*, which are used for special tasks with particular programs; some keys (such as ESCAPE, SHIFT and CONTROL) are used in combination (by being pressed simultaneously) with other keys for other special functions; there are keys for deleting characters, and one for beginning a new line and sending the previous one to the computer. Most keyboards also have keys with arrows on (*cursor keys*) for moving the cursor about the screen so that what you type can be made to appear in different places. The monitor is sometimes called a *VDU* (visual display unit).

This introduction to some of the fundamental concepts should have given you enough information to understand the ideas in the subsequent chapters, but each chapter will give you advice about further reading.

2 Using Large Text Data-banks on Computers

LEE DAVIDSON

INTRODUCTION

Recently a student whose mother tongue was not English asked me how the verb 'need' is used in English. She had noticed that people sometimes say things like, 'He needn't come' as well as 'He needs a haircut', and that 'Need we go?' can occur as well as 'Do we need to go?'. I was able to tell her some of the information which grammatical descriptions of English give about this verb: that it has uses as an auxiliary verb like 'can' and 'may', but is not used in the full range of grammatical constructions that these verbs are found in; that some speakers might prefer 'Do we need to go' to 'Need we go' in conversational English and so on. In the past this is as far as I could have gone with such a question. I certainly could not ask the student to go away and read 2.5 million words of English, noting down all the uses of 'need'. But with modern technology it was a good opportunity to use a *computer corpus* of English language texts to help throw further light on how this verb is used. A computer corpus (from the Latin word for 'body') is a large collection of samples of written or spoken language, specially prepared for use on a computer, containing perhaps as many as 1 million words or more, which can be searched by the computer much faster than a human reader could ever read the same amount of text on the printed page. In fact, in this case it was the work of a few minutes to prepare searches in three such corpora which are widely used in English language research by computer: the Lancaster–Oslo/Bergen corpus of written British English (always referred to as LOB) and the Brown corpus of written US English which both contain 1 million words, and the London–Lund corpus of spoken English which contains about 0.5 million words. In 'What do the corpora look like and why?' below we shall look at some short extracts from these corpora and consider how they have been prepared as electronic documents. Even with modern computer technology the answers to the questions did not come back instantaneously. The computer and the program I used took 21 minutes 45 seconds running time to go through all three corpora and find for me a total of 1495 examples of the words 'need', 'needs', 'needing' and 'needed'.

How did I extract the examples from the corpora? I used a standard computer 'package' called the *Oxford Concordance Program* (discussed in 'The Oxford Concordance Program' below, p. 23) to find and display on the page all the examples of the verbs which were found in the corpora. Each occurrence of the verb was shown in a few lines of surrounding context, like this:

```
A 20 62   k an emergency standstill agreement with the Russians on the Berlin
situation alone as a first step to broader negotiations. ↑This could be
informal in the sense that no document need be signed. *<*4Short-term Basis*>
| ↑*0It could be reached a
```

Using these examples I was able to show the student something of the actual range of uses of the verb.

WHAT DO THE CORPORA LOOK LIKE AND WHY?

First we need to know a little about what a corpus of texts looks like and why it does not always look like ordinary printed language.

The LOB corpus

Here are the opening few lines of the LOB corpus:

```
A01   1 **[001 TEXT A01**]
A01   2 *<*'*7STOP ELECTING LIFE PEERS**'*>
A01   3 *<*4By TREVOR WILLIAMS*>
A01   4   |↑A *0MOVE to stop \0Mr. Gaitskell from nominating any more Labour
A01   5 life Peers is to be made at a meeting of Labour 0{M P}s tomorrow.
A01   6   |↑\0Mr. Michael Foot has put down a resolution on the subject and
A01   7 he is to be backed by \0Mr. Will Griffiths,   0M P   for Manchester
A01   8 Exchange.
```

You may need some persuading that this is a piece of newspaper English! First let us take the material on the left of each line:

```
A01   1
A01   2
A01   3
        ... etc
```

This is called *reference material* and tells me that this bit of text comes from the category A texts in LOB (newspaper reportage – there are 14 other categories), that I am looking at text 1 in that category (there are 44) and that I am looking at lines 1 to 8 of that text which is 2000 words long. Every one of over 100,000 lines in the corpus contains information like this which my searching programs can use to navigate through the corpus. For example, I might only want to examine texts in category B, or to look at lines 1 to 10 of the first 50 texts in the corpus. The references will enable me to do this. If I find words during my computer searches I want to know exactly where the words I have found occur in the corpus. This would be impossible without attaching reference material to the text, just as an index to a book would be useless if the printer had forgotten to give the pages numbers.

The first line is just a boundary marker, put in at the very beginning of the text. Everything else represents the text proper. What you can see here is a headline, a by-line (reporter's name) and the first four lines of a news story. But of course it does not look very much like a page of a newspaper; there is no large typeface for the headline, and the layout has disappeared – or so it seems. If I look up the manual which tells me how this corpus was prepared, I will find what the extra bits and pieces mixed up with the words do:

*< and *> in line 2 mark a headline in the original, and the same markers are used in line 3 to mark the by-line.

*7 in line 2 marks the start of italic bold typeface.

*4 in line 3 marks the start of bold typeface.

*0 in line 4 marks the start of ordinary lower case.

| marks the beginning of a paragraph.

↑ marks the beginning of a new sentence.

\0 shows that Mr. is a contracted word.

So indirectly, through a quite elaborate set of coded markers, all of which use ordinary characters which can be found on any computer keyboard and VDU screen, I can reconstruct to quite a considerable extent what the original page looked like. If, as an investigator, I ever wanted to find out how many headlines in the LOB corpus were originally printed in italic bold I could find the answer. Notice also that the later examples on the list of coding features represent linguistic features such as sentence boundaries rather than typographical information. This is used for the kinds of investigation you will learn more about in '"And" and "but" at the beginning of sentences' on page 20. The corpus manual also tells me that this piece of text came from the *Daily Herald* of 7 February 1961.

The price that has to be paid for this kind of information is that the text in its electronic form becomes less and less readable by a human reader. But then it was not designed for that purpose. The user of the corpus will be using some program to interrogate the corpus which will 'clean up' the coding if required.

This corpus contains many other encoding conventions, which make it a most useful source of information about written English. Some information from the original texts has been discarded, though. We can no longer see where the newspaper stories were divided into columns. The corpus editors decided that was not likely to be relevant for the sort of linguistic research they were preparing the corpus for. For example, the algebraic equations which peppered the extracts from technical documents in a later section of the corpus were omitted, leaving only a marker to show where they occurred.

The tagged LOB corpus

For linguistic research which goes beyond counting occurrences of written forms, the version of LOB we have just seen does not offer much direct assistance to the investigator. The written form 'bear', for example, corresponds to more than one dictionary word: the noun which is both the name of an animal and a particular kind of dealer on the Stock Exchange, and a verb with several distinct meanings. How far can a corpus go in distinguishing different words? A second stage of the work on LOB involved attaching grammatical information to each word – a process called tagging – so that it would then be possible to distinguish 'orders' as a plural noun from 'orders' as third person singular present of the verb. Tagging is a process which can be carried out by a computer, but not especially easily and needs a program which is not readily available.

The principle of tagging, however, is an important one. We can choose to attach information to the words we think need to be distinguished in some way as we type in the text. So we make sure that all forms such as 'MP' are marked as contracted forms (leave aside the homonymy problem of Member of Parliament and Military Police) by surrounding them with special marking characters such as {MP} which are not going to be used for any other purpose. A full-scale tagging system to provide grammatical information about every word in the text would have to have a set of codes which could be attached to the words to represent a chosen set of grammatical distinctions. So 'who' when used as a relative pronoun in 'the man who came to dinner' might be tagged who_REL while 'who' as an interrogative marker in 'who came?' would be coded as who_INT .

Here is a tagged version of the same lines from LOB which we saw earlier:

```
A01  2 *'_*' stop_VB electing_VBG life_NN peers_NNS **'_**' ._.
A01  3 ↑ by_IN Trevor_NP Williams_NP ._.
A01  4 | ↑ a_AT move_NN to_TO stop_VB \0Mr_NPT Gaitskell_NP from_IN
A01  4 nominating_VBG any_DTI more_AP labour_NN
A01  5 life_NN peers_NNS is_BEZ to_TO be_BE made_VBN at_IN a_AT meeting_NN
A01  5 of_IN labour_NN \0MPs_NPTS tomorrow_NR ._.
A01  6 | ↑ \0Mr_NPT Michael_NP Foot_NP has_HVZ put_VBN down_RP a_AT
A01  6 resolution_NN on_IN the_ATI subject_NN and_CC
A01  7 he_PP3A is_BEZ to_TO be_BE backed_VBN by_IN \0Mr_NPT Will_NP
A01  7 Griffiths_NP ,_, \0MP_NPT for_IN Manchester_NP
A01  8 Exchange_NP ._.
```

This is even less readable than untagged LOB. It takes up more space, because there is more information. The reference material on the left is as before. Every word is followed by a tag connected by the character _. In the first line 'stop' is coded VB which means that it is the basic form of a verb. In line 3 'move' is coded NN which means it is a singular common noun. In this way it is distinguished from occurrences of 'move_VB', the verb. This corpus clears up a large amount of the ambiguity of forms in English. (The word spelled 'round' can be a verb, a noun, an adjective, a preposition and an adverb.) Notice also that the punctuation receives tags: these are used in further grammatical analysis of the corpus. In ' "Be" and "get" passives' (page 17) we shall see how this information can be used to look for examples of a particular grammatical construction.

The London–Lund corpus of spoken English
This section shows short extracts from the London–Lund corpus of spoken English which consists of many pieces of *unrehearsed speech*, including conversations (some bugged), telephone calls, and unscripted broadcast talk. An explanation of some of the information which each line contains follows. The encoding system is complex and the corpus is even less immediately readable than the LOB corpus (though there is a printed version of the conversational parts of

the corpus which uses a more readable set of conventions).[1] The main things to remember as you look at it are that unrehearsed speech consists of 'turns' by each speaker rather than paragraphs. In principle it is more like a play, but much 'messier' because, in real life, utterances contain interruptions and the like. There is no unit corresponding to the sentence in speech, but what is marked very carefully are the 'prosodic' features of the utterances – intonation (movements of pitch) and stress (more forcibly marked syllables). Selections of these features characterise different types of 'tone unit', which you can think of as the nearest equivalent to a sentence in this kind of language.

```
1 2   1   10 1 1 A    11 1it went off 1very very !sm\oothly#              /
1 2   1   20 2 1 A    21 1*((at))*                          /
1 2   1   30 1 1 B    11 1*1ah\a#*                          /
1 2   1   20 1 1 (A   11 1that 1meeting of the executive com:m\ittee#     /
1 2   1   40 1 1 A    11 1((3 to 4 sylls)) *-* and I 1r\ang you# **-**    /
1 2   1   50 1 1 A    11 1on the 1way to the /air_port# -             /
1 2   1   60 1 1 A    11 1and +[@:m]+ 1you were /out#               /
1 2   1   70 1 1 B    11 1*1y\es#*                          /
1 2   1   80 1 1 B    11 1**1y\es#**                        /
1 2   1   90 1 1 B    11 1+1that was /it#+                       /
1 2   1   100 1 2 (A  11 1but 1then came and !j\oined ((you)) at the     /
1 2   1   100 1 1 (A  11 111=air_port#1#                        /
1 2   1   110 1 1 A   21 1and 1said *((sylls))*                   /
1 2   1   120 1 1 B   11 1*((1this was [@sw] was))* "!very c\urious#      /
1 2   1   130 2 1 B   22 11all this *[@] -* ((4 to 5 sylls)) . we'd       /
1 2   1   140 1 1 A   11 1*1y\es#                           /
1 2   1   150 1 1 A   11 11y\es#*                           /
1 2   1   130 1 1 (B  12 1((1already)) h/\ad the _meeting#             /
1 2   1   160 1 1 B   11 11with the four con:f\essors#               /
1 2   1   170 1 2 B   12 1((at)) which they'd 1been in ((at)) 1which !Carter /
1 2   1   170 1 1 B   12 1and ((:P\/eel)) *had* _said# .            /
1 2   1   180 1 1 A   11 1*1y=es#*                          /
1 2   2   190 1 1 (B  11 11y\eah# *.*                          /
```

As with the LOB corpus, some material is encoded in fixed columns on the left.

1. Columns 1 to 10 contain the main reference system.

2. Columns 11 to 13 show the tone unit number. Ignoring the '0', you will see

---

[1] R. Quirk and J. Svartvik. *A Corpus of English Conversation*. Lund: Gleerup, 1980.

that tone unit 2 is split into two because another bit of speech comes in the middle.

3. Columns 18 to 19 show you who is speaking (A or B). The character '(' in front of the letter shows that it is the continuation of an interrupted turn.

4. The remaining columns tell you how to fit the bits of different tone units together.

Within the text proper, a whole forest of markers is found, of which the following are the more important ones:

1. / and \ are used singly and in combination to show rises and falls of pitch on the syllables which are intonationally important.

2. ↑ and # mark the beginning and ending, more or less, of a tone unit.

3. ((...)) surround words which the transcribers could not hear properly on the tape. In some cases they guess a word, but in others they are able only to say how many syllables were uttered.

4. [...] surround all sorts of 'phonetic' material – half finished words, filler noises like 'er' and 'um' and so on.

5. * and + are used to show which utterances overlapped in the original conversation.

So, not only can we find out what words the speakers uttered but we can also, if we need to, look at important information-carrying devices like pitch which simply do not occur in writing. Look at the word 'yes' which occurs six times in the extract: five times as 'yes' and once as 'yeah'. Five of these occurrences have falling pitch, but one has level pitch (marked by the = character in front of the vowel). Is that what you would expect to find in these examples? When 'yes' is being used to show the speaker is, more or less, going along with what the other person is saying, is a fall or level pitch the only one possible? Say the word 'yes' to yourself with a rise and ask yourself where it would be found. Notice also that the 'yes' words are not being used to answer questions. Is this the way they are normally used in conversation? Such important questions about how we use a very common word in real speech can only begin to be answered when we have something like this corpus.

Other corpora

The two corpora we have seen (one in two versions) are the ones which are used in Britain most often for research, but we should not forget the pioneering Brown corpus of American written English which was the model for LOB and was produced by W. Nelson Francis and H. Kučera at Brown University back in the 1960s before computers became widespread. It is very similar in appearance to LOB, and contains 500 extracts of 2000 words from the same 15 different varieties of written English published in the USA in 1961. Other corpora of English language material include the Lancaster/IBM Spoken English corpus (about 52,000 words of contemporary spoken English available in various formats, some with intonation and tagging), the Helsinki corpus of English texts (1.5 million words of Old, Middle and Early Modern English), and the Kohlapur corpus (1 million words of printed Indian English). Professor Sidney Greenbaum is in charge of a large project to produce the International Corpus of English, which will cover English from many parts of the world. There are already some corpora available from Australia, and a New Zealand corpus is under way. Early in 1991 the British National Corpus project was announced, which will ultimately make available a very large corpus of around 100 million words.

Large corpora exist for other languages. There is a rough equivalent of LOB for German, and the *Trésor de la Langue Française* project in France has amassed a gigantic database, primarily for lexicographic work on French, from which data can be extracted for use by other scholars. The *Thesaurus Linguae Graecae* project covering Classical and later Greek texts is mentioned below. The important Biblical Hebrew texts are available in machine-readable form, and a corpus of Modern Hebrew has been started. There is recent news of corpus-based studies starting in Japan. Doubtless there are many other corpora which have been built up to serve the purposes of particular research groups. There is a continuing difficult problem with copyright which affects almost all modern material, and makes the inclusion of complete texts in databases unattractive to commercial publishers who often own the copyright of modern texts.

Can machines save us retyping texts?

Constructing any corpus is a huge and expensive task. There are machines called optical character readers (OCR) which can scan a page of text (often, alas, only when the book has been removed from its binding) and decide what letters it has seen and turn them into a computer file without having to retype the text at a keyboard. But it has to be said that they are often inaccurate, and require a skilled operator to keep the error count low. If an OCR finds a lower-case 'e' with a faint or missing bar, it will decide it is seeing 'c'. It cannot recognise that 'thc' for 'the' is nonsense. The file which is produced is just like a bare version of what was on the page. All the reference and other encoded material still has to be added. So do not get the idea that OCRs make corpus production easy.

WHAT CAN WE USE CORPORA FOR?

Students of language might want to use a corpus for any of the following:

1. Counting frequencies of words and comparing frequencies in different sorts of text (e.g. newspapers contrasted with novels).

2. Finding all occurrences of a word in a certain amount of surrounding context, such as the sentence in which it occurs, in order to study its uses.

3. Finding all occurrences of a word playing a particular grammatical role (e.g. 'to' as a preposition but not as a marker of the infinitive form of the verb as in 'to see').

4. Tracing relationships between pairs of words or *collocational* relations. For example, if you give English speakers the word 'immemorial' and ask them what words they would expect to occur nearby, it is quite likely that a good number will come up with 'time' because the phrase 'time immemorial' is a cliché. A smaller number perhaps might come up with 'elms' from Tennyson's line 'The moan of doves in immemorial elms'. A good many perhaps would come up with nothing because they had never met the word before. This is a word which has a restricted range of collocations. Linguists are interested in studying this kind of knowledge which speakers have of their language and corpora can provide more examples (though often very large amounts of text are needed).

5. Finding out how often and in what kinds of text borrowed foreign expressions occur, e.g. 'bon appétit', or 'nil desperandum'.

6. Measuring sentence length (in words) and sentence complexity (number of clauses, say) in different kinds of text.

7. Investigating points of English usage on which the practice of speakers and writers is known to be variable, for example how often 'The committee was in agreement...' would occur as against 'The committee were in agreement...'.

The answers to such questions are of interest to students studying language, to translators, to language teachers, in fact to anyone interested in language. Vast sums of money are spent by commercial organisations in establishing what kinds of jam we prefer on our bread, but the language we use every day is rather less well studied. Is it important and necessary to find out what people actually *do* say and write? There is a school of thought which says that all we need to know about are the 'rules' of 'Standard English' grammar and spelling, from which the real performances of speakers and writers are likely to depart in various undesirable ways. Students of language cannot share that view, but they must grant that it has been influential in our culture and has to some extent played a part in inhibiting linguistic research. We know that usage changes through time; to study this we surely need better evidence than casual observation. The founder of the Survey of English Usage, Professor Sir Randolph Quirk, stated the need for large corpora in language study well in 1960:[2]

> The basis [of the survey] must be copious materials, made up of continuous stretches or 'texts' taken from the full range of co-existing varieties and strata of educated English, spoken as well as written, at the present time.

Using corpora opens up possibilities for several kinds of linguistic research. We have seen how a question about grammatical usage in English might be approached; now we will consider some other questions which might come up. These are very like some of the projects which I have worked on with students in the past few years. (In some of the examples which follow, you will be looking at pieces of the corpora which may contain encoding details which are unexplained. Just concentrate on the words proper. Some of the examples will begin and end with incomplete sentences: the bit which is relevant will be in the middle.)

Countable and uncountable uses of nouns in English
Grammarians distinguish 'countable' and 'uncountable' nouns in English (sometimes the terms 'count' and 'mass' are used instead). A countable noun is

---

[2] R. Quirk. 'The Survey of British English', in *Essays on the English Language: Medieval and Modern.* London: Longman, 1968, p. 78.

one like 'boy' or 'book' which has singular and plural forms and can be used in expressions like

the boy read books

I saw a boy and a book

Uncountable nouns are ones like 'hydrogen' or 'happiness' where expressions such as

?? we experienced happinesses

?? I use a hydrogen

which correspond to the previous examples are very odd English indeed. The first group of nouns we can think of as typically naming 'things' and the second 'substances'. The two groups have several different grammatical properties. So far, I have suggested that the two groups are distinct in membership, but this is not so. Consider

He has an egg on his tie

He has egg on his tie

The former must mean either that he has a picture of an egg on his tie or (somewhat less likely) that a real egg is in some way perching on his tie. The second means that there are traces of egg-substance on his tie. The first usage is pretty clearly a countable one, the second uncountable. Are we to conclude that there are different usages of the same noun, or that there are two nouns, one uncountable and the other uncountable? The problem is not easy to solve in a satisfactory way, but if we leave the neatest analysis on one side we can still ask how often in English 'egg' is used in each of the two ways. Many substance nouns such as 'coffee' or 'sugar' can be used in what I shall call a 'type of' sense, as in

The researcher used three different sugars in that series of experiments.

Show me a naturally occurring sugar which we cannot synthesize!

You will notice that the word 'sugar' occurs first in the plural, and secondly with the indefinite article 'a'. This is not the predicted behaviour of an uncountable noun, so we must conclude that something slightly unusual but perfectly grammatical is going on. In certain contexts (e.g. organic chemistry) 'sugar' can be used to refer to any one of a large class of chemical substances apart from the one some of us still put in tea and coffee. Which reminds us that 'sugar' could be used in yet another range of countable ways, as in

The head waiter ordered him to put the sugars on the tables for afternoon tea.

I take two sugars in tea.

A speaker of English will easily be able to give you examples of these various usages but is likely to find it hard to say which occurs most frequently. I used the LOB corpus to throw some light on the question of frequency. I searched for all occurrences of a list of words including 'sugar', 'tea', 'coffee', 'wood', etc. which are known to occur in both uncountable and countable usages. It was *not* possible to ask the computer to distinguish the two types of usage easily, because there is no single clue in the surrounding text which can be linked with one type of noun or the other. Even the tagged version of LOB would simply mark them all as nouns, so the best that could be done was to find all the examples of the words studied and to look at them in enough context to be able to decide what the usage was in each case. The advantage this time of using the computer may seem rather limited, but it is still much faster than looking more or less at random through a pile of books and newspapers, say, picking out every occurrence of 'sugar' or 'coffee' and noting down the surrounding words. Three corpora (LOB, Brown and London–Lund) were searched, and the resulting concordances analysed. As each example was looked at, a tally was kept of what the usage was. Some interesting features emerged.

I shall discuss just one of the words – tea – in the LOB corpus. There were 112 uses of 'tea' and 6 of 'teas'. This in itself tells us that a possible usage of a possessive form, such as 'this tea's flavour is truly remarkable', does not occur at all in the corpus. First there were contexts where it was easy to decide that the usage was uncountable, as in

H 21 104 the interests of the countries and territories associated with the Community. ↑For example, tea is a commodity of great importance to India and Ceylon, and so is cocoa to Ghana. ↑A zero common tariff

Among the 112 uses of 'tea' there was no single example of the 'type of' usage 'this is a tea we ought to be marketing' but there were 2 such uses with 'teas'. Here is one example in context

```
E 26 152 the matter satisfactorily settled once and for all. ↑This applies to
both Indian and China teas. ↑If of the latter you like a *' smoky**' blend,
mention the fact when you ask advice. ↑I do not know how
```

What did turn up was another usage, where 'tea' is the name of a meal, as in

```
G 04 8    a walk over the fields while we attended to our business. ↑To my
amusement, when we met at tea at the rectory after the Dedication, the
Archbishop said he had been stopped by a farmer in a field.
```

This usage is actually quite tricky to distinguish in all cases from other uses, but in the event there were 30 uses of this with 'tea' and 4 with 'teas'. Should this count as countable or uncountable? Surely the former. In this case it is the most frequently occurring countable use of 'tea'/'teas'. There were another 15 cases where 'tea' occurred in a modifying role as in 'tea merchant' and 'The Assam Frontier Tea Company'. Perhaps these should also be considered as uncountable (but would one treat 'tea rooms' as an occurrence of the name of the meal rather than of the commodity?).

The figures presented here provide strong support for the view that the typical behaviour of the noun 'tea' is as an uncountable noun, but as you can see, some interesting problems come up in analysing what the computer extracts from just one corpus. We get confirmation of what our intuitions about the word would probably tell us, but we also identify some new problems in noun classification which even quite large grammars of English rarely if ever discuss.

Sometimes I found examples of usages which I would have hesitated to invent for myself if asked to think about a word. If asked whether 'distress' could be used in countable contexts I believe that many speakers would say no. In LOB I found 18 occurrences of the singular form, all clearly uncountable or like 'distress rockets', but in addition I came up with an example of 'distresses'

```
G 46 173    a nobleman of fine character who was to prove one of her most
faithful friends in all the distresses of her life. ↑In 1780 the chapel was
wrecked in the Gordon Riots. ↑It is usually assumed that the
```

'Be' and 'get' passives

A typical passive construction in English is 'He was promoted last week' but this could also be expressed as 'He got promoted last week'. The version with 'got' is grammatically sound, though you may feel that it does not mean quite the same as the 'was' version, and that it is more colloquial. The verb 'get' used to be, and probably still is, considered to be a 'weak' word to use and I can remember being instructed at school not to use it where an alternative could be found. Despite these views about the verb it is still there, and is used in some apparently passive constructions, but how often?

Searching in the corpora for evidence about passives was quite a challenge, because passive constructions are not, of course, clearly marked, and though it is reasonably easy to say that a passive construction is marked by an occurrence of the auxiliary 'be' in some form followed by a past participle of a verb, the distance between these is unpredictable, as in the made-up example

Their team was, without a shadow of a doubt, soundly defeated

The two items 'was...' and '...defeated' which form the passive verb phrase are widely separated by other words. So a search for a range of expressions composed of a form of the verb 'be' followed immediately by a word ending in '-ed' would capture examples such as 'was defeated' or 'is marked' but would miss the example above. Furthermore, there is the problem of verbs with irregular past participles not ending in '-ed' such as 'hewn' or 'put', though these are fixed in number and can be listed.

This was an opportunity to use the *tagged LOB corpus*. In this version of the corpus every form such as 'hewn', 'defeated', etc. which actually is a past participle form is tagged VBN. A past tense form 'defeated' (as in 'Harry defeated Bill in three sets') would be tagged VBD. So one of the problems, that of specifying what to search for, is dealt with. It was easy to find all occurrences of past participles. It was also easy to pin down all parts of the verb 'be', which have various tags such as BE for 'be', BED for 'were', etc. The remaining problem of unpredictable distance between the auxiliary verb and the past participle cannot easily be solved, so the search was based on an arbitrary assumption that the two words could lie up to four words apart. It was hoped that this would capture a reasonable number of passives, though it would exclude examples such as the one shown above with much intervening material. In the event, so many examples were found that the search had to be restricted to every fifth text in the corpus, i.e. 20% of the total corpus. These texts were evenly distributed throughout all the categories of text. Even so, 2827 examples representing 1622 different expressions were found. If we assume that the other 75% of the corpus contained 'be' Passives at the same level, we could estimate that we would find a total of 14,135 occurrences, exemplifying 8110 distinct expressions. Some of these were bound to be chance occurrences of 'be' followed by a past participle, but as these could only be excluded by examining every context by eye, I shall not attempt to estimate the margin of error. These figures make it clear that this type of passive is very common.

A similar search for any part of 'get' followed by a past participle at up to four words away was also made. In this case the number of occurrences of a part of 'get' followed by a past participle was so limited that it was easy to deal with every example. OCP came up with 149 apparent examples representing 95 different expressions. Of these, 17 turned out to be occurrences of irrelevant constructions, leaving only 132 cases to be examined as 'get' passives. At once a construction emerged which looked like a passive, but differed from a 'be' passive by having an object between the auxiliary and the main verb. Here is a good example:

```
        get_VB squashed_VBN     1

K 11 146  _IN her_PP3O ,_, *'_*' you_PP2 'd_HVD better_RBR
move_VB a_AT bit_NN or_CC you_PP2 'll_MD get_VB your_PP$
pretty_JJ self_NN squashed_VBN flat_JJ !_! **'_**'
| | she_PP3A gave_VBD no_ATI sign_NN tha
```

If you consider 'You will be squashed flat', a 'be' passive sentence, you cannot put anything like 'your pretty self' between the words 'be' and 'squashed', which is precisely what is happening in the example above from the corpus. No less than 36 examples of this turned up, and cannot be strictly compared with 'be' passives. Of the 83 examples of real passives left, 25 were accounted for by occurrences of 'get married' and 22 by 'get rid (of)'. You may well feel that this last example should really be excluded because it is not a true passive – for example it will not readily convert back into an active version. In this case the number of 'get' passives drops to 61. Here are two good examples:

```
        gets_VBZ heated_VBN     1

E 26 160  NNS  are_BER not_XNOT always_RB properly_RB observed_VBN ;_;
perhaps_RB the_ATI teapot_NN gets_VBZ heated_VBN with_IN hot_JJ water_NN
,_, but_CC is_BEZ not_XNOT subsequently_RB completely_RB emptie
```

```
        gets_VBZ misused_VBN     1

G 11 7  _NN ._. | did_DOD they_PP3AS know_VB how_WRB wealth_NN from_IN over-
large_JJ estates_NNS gets_VBZ misused_VBN ?_? | they_PP3AS 'd_HVD heard_VBN
of_IN great_JJ estates_NNS being_BEG enclosed_VBN in_
```

It is a pity that we do not have more space here to look at the 'get' passives more closely, but one property which they appear to have is of some interest. Here is a list of the main verbs involved:

> blamed, blocked, bogged down, burned, broken, caught, dragged in, entangled, heated, held up, hit, hurt, left, lost, misused, nicked, paid, picked up, re-elected, scraped, spliced, snapped up, trained, upset

Does it not strike you that the meanings of most, though not all, of these verbs fall into a category one might loosely call 'unpleasant fate', where something undesirable has happened to the person who underwent the experience? I remember feeling this quite strongly when investigating these passives before I had access to a corpus, and was interested to see my hunch borne out by the data from LOB. More seriously, it will be obvious that 'get' passives are quite rare, at any rate in the kinds of written English represented in LOB. These passives seem to be restricted to just a few verbs and to have elements in their meaning which are not found in regular 'be' passives. Comparisons with the London-Lund corpus of spoken English would be required to see if they are more frequent in spoken English.

'And' and 'but' at the beginning of sentences

Traditional teaching of English dislikes beginning a sentence with 'and'. To a certain extent this disfavour extends to 'but' as well. Fowler's *English Usage*, for example, says of 'and' beginning a sentence:

> That it is a solecism to begin a sentence with *and* is a faintly lingering superstition. The OED [*Oxford English Dictionary*] gives examples ranging from the 10th to the 19th c.; the Bible is full of them.[3]

This confirms that some disapprove of using 'and' in this position, but that it was not one of the popular views about usage which Fowler was prepared to support. What does the LOB corpus tell us? In the first place, the corpus editors have performed a great service by actually marking the beginning of each sentence. Why did they bother to do this? Surely writing conventions such as the use of

---

[3] H.W. Fowler (revised Sir E. Gowers). *A Dictionary of Modern English Usage*. Oxford: Clarendon Press, 1965.

full-stop are enough. In fact it turns out to be quite hard to decide where sentence divisions come in written English in a significant number of cases. Direct speech in novels is a tricky problem, for example. Do you count all the 'he saids' as sentences which are distinct from the words actually spoken by the character? Punctuation is often inconsistent in such cases. So LOB sentences are marked on a consistent basis. The investigation used the information that every sentence beginning is marked with the character 'ʇ' to find the cases where the first word is 'and' or 'but'. The program used was not the Oxford Concordance Program, which would not have counted the number of sentences very conveniently, but a program written in the Spitbol programming language. The program converted the entire corpus to sentences, looked at the beginning of each sentence and kept a count of the number of times in each of the 500 texts in the corpus that a sentence began with one or other of the words.

First of all, I found that both words are distributed through all the kinds of text in the corpus, but initial 'but' with 1547 examples is considerably more frequent than 'and' with 875. Given that each of the 500 excerpts in LOB is 2000 words long it is easy to work out the average number of cases per text over the whole corpus: 1.75 occurrences of 'and', and 3.09 occurrences of 'but'. But there are quite striking differences between different *categories* of text. There are 15 different categories of text in the corpus, ranging from journalism through technical and scientific writing to pulp fiction. We do not have space to look at all the figures, but the maximum and minimum occurrences of the two words are set out in Table 1.

Table 1: Maximum and minimum occurrences of sentence-initial 'and' and 'but' in LOB

	AND				BUT			
	min		max		min		max	
categ	rate	categ	rate	categ	rate	categ	rate
H	0.07	M	3.83	H	1.30	M	6.83

H = Miscellaneous (government documents, reports, etc.)
M = Science fiction

Interestingly, it turns out that science fiction texts make by far the most use of both initial 'and' and 'but'; a miscellaneous group which includes government reports, industry reports and company accounts is at the other end of the spectrum. Why this should be so is, of course, another question. The level in fictional texts tends to be above average, but finding why this is so would have involved looking closely at the specific examples. When we look at the occurrences in individual texts, we find some surprising differences again. The text with most initial 'and' has 25 examples, but it turns out that most of these occur in quoted passages of Biblical language, so they are certainly not typical of modern English. This also fits in with what Fowler says, but I do not think that modern speakers or writers would be happy to use initial 'and' as often as it occurs in the Bible. This raises the question of why the usage should be disapproved of if it occurs in the Authorised Version of the Bible – otherwise normally regarded as a model of English style. As you can see, the issues are becoming more complicated. This is a good example of the stimulus to research which corpus investigations provide.

'Hopefully'
One of the most controversial usages in English today is that which is exemplified by

Hopefully, the match will be over before the rain starts.

More ink has been spilt on this usage than on almost any other single feature of 'slipping' English usage. There are many explanations for its appearance and growth, usually blaming the USA. So can we use the LOB and Brown corpora to throw light on possible US origins for this usage? There is a problem that the texts in both corpora were published in 1961, which is earlier than the fuss about 'hopefully'. Nevertheless, I looked through both corpora for the word, and found 8 occurrences in Brown (US English) and 11 in LOB (British English). In 18 cases the usage is 'innocent', by which I mean that it represents a non-controversial use of the word – the range of uses which those who write the letters to the BBC think should be the only uses for this word. Here is one example from LOB:

```
A 10 12   prodded the turf and announced that the going
would be *"a little soft.**" IBut he looked hopefully at the sky and
guessed that all would come well. *<*6LUNCHCONTEST*> I*0All did.
```

But one of the examples in Brown is different. Significantly it comes from a newspaper report, and newspapers are often the earliest places where new usages emerge in print.

```
A 37 179 p their slim majority and prepared to choke
off debate on the filibuster battle this week. Hopefully,
```

the perennial battle of Rule 22 then would be fought to a settlement once and for all.

So we get very modest support for the idea that this feature is one which comes from US usage. What we need, obviously, is a much larger and more historically representative corpus.

HOW DO WE GET INFORMATION OUT OF A CORPUS?

In this section we will look at ways of getting the corpus to reveal its secrets – computer programs which can be used to 'read' through the huge file, find words, count them, remember which texts and lines they occurred in, and possibly store the context in which they occurred.

The Oxford Concordance Program

One of the most widely used packages for the analysis of text corpora is the Oxford Concordance Program.[4] This makes it easy to produce three different kinds of listing of words from a machine-readable text: *wordlists, indexes* and *concordances.* Here is a very short text, prepared for use with OCP.

```
<A ECBentley>
The Art of Biography
Is different from Geography.
Geography is about Maps,
But Biography is about Chaps.
```

The first line contains the author's name in a widely used format for placing reference material in electronic documents – COCOA format references. We use the letter A to mean 'author's name', and attach E.C. Bentley's name in a compact form. The pointed brackets round the reference mean that OCP will not treat them as part of the text. COCOA references (named after the ancestor of

---

[4] The current version for mainframe computers runs on very many machines, and there is a version *Micro OCP* for use on PCs. The package is fully described in S. Hockey and J. Martin. *Oxford Concordance Package: User's Manual Version 2*, Oxford University Computing Service, 1988.

OCP) are commonly used in preparing literary texts electronically. Here is an OCP *wordlist* of all the words in this text, listing all the words sorted in alphabetical order with their frequencies and some summary statistics at the end.

```
about                    2
Art                      1
Biography                2
But                      1
Chaps                    1
different                1
from                     1
Geography                2
Is                       3
Maps                     1
of                       1
The                      1
```

```
TOTAL WORDS READ      =    17
TOTAL WORDS SELECTED  =    17
TOTAL WORDS PICKED    =    17
TOTAL WORDS SAMPLED   =    17
TOTAL WORDS KEPT      =    17
TOTAL VOCABULARY      =    12
```

Now here are the first four entries from an *index* of the same text. This time as well as frequencies for the words (the first figure after each word), an abbreviated author's name and the line number locations of all occurrences of the words are given.

```
about    2   ECBen 3, ECBen 4

Art    1   ECBen 1

Biography    2   ECBen 1, ECBen 4

But    1   ECBen 4
...
```

And now here are the corresponding entries from a *concordance*, which lists all the words with their frequencies and in addition shows each occurrence of each word in the context of the line where it occurs. Author's name and line number are on the left.

```
                        about    2
ECBen 3         Geography is about Maps
ECBen 4      But Biography is about Chaps


                        Art    1
ECBen 1         The Art of Biography


                     Biography    2
ECBen 1         The Art of Biography
ECBen 4             But Biography is about Chaps


                        But    1
ECBen 4         But Biography is about Chaps
```

How does the user of OCP get it to produce such listings of words?

OCP command files

The user must have access to whichever corpus is to be used. The OCP program provides a large range of commands which, when applied to the text, will perform various tasks such as identifying the words, counting frequencies, and arranging the words nicely for printing. The user makes up a small computer 'file' containing the commands needed for the job, then 'runs' the OCP package by telling it to execute these commands on a particular text. The OCP program goes through the text and performs whatever tasks it has been instructed to do in the command file. Here is the command file which was used to produce the concordance of the small text we looked at above.

```
*input
references cocoa.
*action
do concordance.
references A = 5, L = 1.
*format
layout width 70.
*go
```

Here are some explanatory comments on this command file:

1. The command file is very short. Just a few commands are given but the job which is done is actually quite complex. (If you have struggled to write your own programs in BASIC, say, you might like to work out how long a program you would have to write to do all the things which OCP did in this job; it would be several hundred lines long to get anywhere near what OCP does. The OCP program behind the scenes which the user never has to know about is many thousands of lines long.) We shall see shortly how OCP has been designed to keep the command files as short as possible.

2. The commands are (mostly) written in quite ordinary English. It is perfectly easy to work out what 'do concordance' is about. It is true that *references cocoa* is a bit mysterious; this command tells the OCP program that the text has been prepared with Cocoa references.

3. The layout of the commands does follow some rules. The lines beginning with * mark different 'sections' which do different jobs, and these have to be in a fixed order. Notice that each separate command ends with a full-stop; if this is omitted OCP will not know what to do with your commands and will report an error. So some care is needed in preparing command files accurately.

4. The command line *references A = 5, L = 1.* controls how the author's name and line numbers will appear on the page.

5. In the **format* section the command *layout width 70* provides for the concordance to be printed on a page which is no more than 70 characters wide.

The reason why you can compose such a short and simple command file and yet get a very elaborate analysis of the words of the text is because OCP does all kinds of jobs in a predetermined way without needing explicit instructions. These are what are usually called 'default' actions. They happen without the user having to ask for them to happen. If the user wants something different to happen then s/he will have to put an appropriate command in the file. That is why the user has to tell OCP nothing about how it is to recognise what words are. All this is provided for by 'defaults' which are built into OCP. This has great advantages for the user.

What can OCP do?

The examples we saw above listed all the words in the short text, but if you are working on a large corpus you would never want all that – the amount of printout would use bales of paper which you would never be able to read. Normally you want to pick a limited set of words or phrases. OCP has neat ways of doing these jobs: here are some examples of commands you can use to get it to look for single words, groups of words and phrases:

```
pick words "need*".
```

This will look for and hold on to all words which begin with the letters 'need-', so we could use this to do the job we started out with, looking for 'needs', 'needed' etc. The * means 'any letter or letters including none at all' following 'need'. It would also find 'needy', 'needless' and so on, which we might not want. All OCP does is look mechanically, but of course very quickly, for any word beginning with the letters requested.

```
include phrases "lay* o*", "set* aside".
```

This would hold onto occurrences of 'lay off', 'lay out', 'laying out', 'sets aside', 'setting aside' and so on.

Most sophisticated of all are searches for 'collocations' like the following:

```
include collocates "lay*" up to 4 "off".
```

This time OCP will look for any of the words 'lay', 'lays' etc. followed by the word 'off' at anywhere up to four words to the right. So this would find an example in the text like 'lay the workforce off', because 'off' occurs three places to the right of 'lay'. This is especially useful for investigating expressions which consist of words separated by other words, like the examples of *phrasal verbs* shown. These two-part verbs are very common in English and normal dictionaries often give very little information about them, so corpora are a valuable source of information. The collocates feature was used in finding the passives we looked at earlier.

OCP not only allows you to pick any words you want to, it permits different kinds of sorting. The obvious (and default) order is normal English alphabetical order from A/a to Z/z where the letters are scanned from left to right within the word. But OCP also allows you to scan the letters from right to left so that words with similar *endings* are close together. The three words 'aardvark', 'middle' and 'zygote' would appear in a normal dictionary in the order given, but if they are sorted from the end of the word, they will appear in the order 'middle', 'zygote', 'aardvark'. To get this order you would simply include in your command file the command

```
keys sorted by end.
```

The wordlist now allows you to see words with similar endings close together. Why would you want to do this? If you were studying the use of particular verb forms, say the ones ending in '-ing' it would be hard to weed them out of a normally sorted list, but in a reverse sorted one the words can be found together. In the Preface to Dr Johnson's *A Dictionary of the English Language* (1755) I find this sentence:

> There is more danger of censure from the multiplicity than
> paucity of examples...

I see here two words ending in '-city'. These are rather academic words, perhaps stereotypically 'Johnsonian'. But how many other such words does he use? A reverse sorted wordlist is the most convenient way I have of finding out (assuming I have an electronic version of Johnson's works).

One of the most important properties of OCP is that it allows you to create limitless alphabets to represent other languages and get the words sorted in the right order. If you only use OCP to examine English texts you never need to put in a command defining an alphabet, but not all languages sort words the same way as we do in English. In Spanish, for example, 'ch' and 'll' count as separate letters of the alphabet (so the word 'churros' for example would appear in the next section of the dictionary quite a long way *after* a word like 'clase'). You can arrange for this kind of sort quite easily using OCP.

Limitations of OCP

OCP is quite easy to use, but it has lots of limitations. Because it looks for 'words' as sequences of letters it cannot distinguish homonyms or any of the tricky cases we looked at earlier unless they have been tagged in some way. Although it produces lots of statistics about word frequencies, it does not allow sentence length to be measured, which is something one often wants to do in stylistic studies. Perhaps most seriously of all, it does not give instant answers if the amount of text to be searched is very large, as is the case with any of the corpora. Even on a very powerful mainframe computer OCP will take around

5 minutes to produce a wordlist which involves picking 10 or 12 words out of the LOB corpus. Of course, this is much faster than you would be able to read through 1 million words of text, but it is not instantaneous. On a small microcomputer, assuming you could get the whole of the LOB corpus onto it, it would take hours to do a job like this. The reason is that the OCP program has to read through the whole text from scratch each time. Although it can be used to produce indexes of texts, it does not store these indexes in its memory. If you want swift retrieval of examples from a large body of material it is normally much more efficient to search an index of the text, find the relevant locations quickly, then go to these locations to find the words of context. OCP works the other way round.

Alternatives to OCP

What I have described so far is the version of OCP as used in a mainframe computing system. The PC version Micro-OCP has several advantages for the beginner, as it is built around menus which take the user through the stages of a job in an orderly fashion and includes a simple and effective editor for creating command files. Two other packages for use on PCs have quite a wide following. Both are fast to use interactively because they work on indexes of the text. These are TACT, which is very cheap, and WordCruncher, which is more expensive. A number of text databases are available in the special format used for WordCruncher.

WRITING YOUR OWN PROGRAMS: SPITBOL AND OTHER LANGUAGES

Text analysis packages are the easiest, and, for many purposes, the best way of getting information out of text corpora. Certainly the common type of interrogation of the corpus to show examples of words or phrases in context is best met in this way. But what can we do when the packages cannot meet the need, because of their inbuilt limitations? Suppose we want to find out something about sentence length, which OCP is unable to calculate? We must then turn to *programming languages* and develop a program to do the job.

There are hundreds of programming languages, though not very many really widely used ones. BASIC is still the best-known language, largely because it was given away free with many of the microcomputers that made computing popular in the 1980s. As far as text-processing is concerned, a language particularly well-suited for that kind of use is SNOBOL4 or more often its child SPITBOL.[5] This is now being displaced by a new language called ICON[6] which has the kind of features which made SPITBOL so useful, but belongs to the age of Artificial Intelligence rather than when computers took up rooms filled with glowing valves.

Programming gives the user a degree of freedom from the limitations of packages. In the real world it can only be a limited freedom. It would be very foolhardy for a user who was fed up with the word-processor on his or her machine to set out to write a new one. The effort would be vast, and it would be cheaper in every sense to buy a new package which had the features the first one did not have. But knowledge of a programming language can give the user the freedom to write small-scale 'tool' programs which can get round the limitations of packages with relatively little effort. This is quite apart from the fact that, for some, programming is an intellectually stimulating activity in which creativity can be exploited in a way never possible with a package.

There has been considerable debate about whether it is worth teaching students who are not computer specialists to program. The main arguments in favour of learning to program are that it tests the student more interestingly than package use does, that it can be a satisfying creative activity even where the programs produced would never have commercial value, and it makes any user realise how much is actually involved in programming and therefore a better judge of what any piece of software can do (or less likely to fall victim to the honeyed words of the next software salesperson). It is very likely that some students will get into programming after graduating, in which case the experience gained in programming as a part of their studies can be important in telling them whether they like programming or not.

This is not the place to try to teach programming, but some idea of what would be involved can be gained by looking at how you might go about writing programs to count the number of words in each sentence in a piece of text using SPITBOL.

Why is SPITBOL better than others? It was specifically designed, in the 1960s, to do what almost no computing language at that time could easily do, namely to process *strings of character data*. Early computer languages were nearly all designed with numerical calculation in mind, and this often made them very inconvenient for performing tasks such as finding patterns in data. If you think

---

[5] R.E. Griswold, J.F. Poage and I.P. Polonsky. *The SNOBOL4 Programming Language.* Englewood Cliffs: Prentice Hall, Inc., 1971.

[6] R.E. and M.T. Griswold. *The ICON Programming Language.* Englewood Cliffs: Prentice Hall, Inc., 2nd edn, 1990.

of words as strings of characters it is fairly clear that you want to be able to do things such as test whether one string of characters is the same as another, or whether string A is found in string B or vice versa and so on. This is different from adding, subtracting and so on which is what you want to do with numbers. SNOBOL4, which was later developed into SPITBOL (from SPeedy ImplemenTation of snoBOL), was created with just such purposes in mind.

Let us follow through a simple example of how a program might work in SPITBOL. The program will find in succession all the words in a small piece of text:

```
The cunning cat, however, continued to sit on
Mary's mat.
```

If we approach this in the most obvious way, namely that each word is a sequence of letters up to but not including a space, we would get words of a kind, but they would be mixed up with punctuation (comma and full stop). There is also the problem of the apostrophe in *Mary's* , which we might think of as punctuation, but is really part of the word here. Here is the central part of a SPITBOL program which would print out a list of words in the text – not sorted:

```
    LETTERS = "ABCDEFGHIJKLMNOPQRSTUVWXYZ"
+           "abcdefghijklmnopqrstuvwxyz'"
    NEXT_LINE LINE = INPUT                        :F(END)
    NEXT_WORD LINE BREAK(LETTERS) SPAN(LETTERS)
+      . WORD =                                   :F(NEXT_LINE)
          OUTPUT = WORD                           :(NEXT_WORD)
    END
```

How does this work? Each line of the program is a command to perform a task. First we define all the characters which will count as letters in words. Notice that this includes after 'z' the character we need in the apostrophe, but excludes the other punctuation. The line beginning NEXT_LINE reads in each line of the text (in our case only two lines) and fills a variable LINE with each line of the text in turn. When there is no more text to read, the program run will end because this operation will 'fail'. The F provides for where to go in case of failure, in this case to the END of the program. The next line is the heart of the program. It uses two special features of the language to find just those sequences of characters which will count as words. BREAK causes the program to look through the string of characters in LINE and to move a scanning 'finger' until it detects one of the characters LETTERS, at which point the scanning finger will stop. This, in effect, jumps over and forgets about all the things which are not letters such as spaces and punctuation. Then SPAN takes over. It starts moving the scanning finger again and this time moves it along as long as it keeps finding what are defined as letters, until it detects that the next character coming up is not defined as a letter and then it stops the finger. At that point all the characters which it has found as it scans are put into a variable called WORD and are then deleted from LINE. So, the first time this works, it would bite off the letters 'The' then stop. If this operation fails, because we have reached the end of this line of the text, the program goes back to NEXT_LINE and gets the next line of the text. If SPAN succeeds in finding a word, however, the program goes on to execute its next command, which is to print (on the screen perhaps) the word just found. The special instruction OUTPUT does this. Then the program goes back and looks for the next word, and so on until in the end the program runs out of lines of text. Then it has done its job and can end.

Many programs like this can be written to perform tasks with the corpora which cannot be performed by a concordancing package such as OCP. One such program – the one mentioned in '"And" and "but" at the beginning of sentences' on page 21 – transforms the LOB corpus into sentences, and a similar program converts the London–Lund corpus into forms where each tone unit is separated or clears the prosodic encoding characters out of the text so that the corpus can be read easily by a human.

SUMMING UP

The availability of corpora has made it possible for students in linguistics departments to carry out investigations on a scale which would have been impossible before in many areas of the subject – grammar, discourse analysis and stylistics. This chapter has tried to show the kinds of material and computer software which can be used now in almost any university. There is a fast growing body of computer readable material, which is made available through national depositories such as the *Oxford Text Archive*. The work of international groups of scholars such as the ICAME (International Computer Archive of Modern English) group is making more and more corpora available. In the case of older languages it is now possible to get virtually all the major authors in machine-readable form. The *Thesaurus Linguae Graecae* project has prepared all Classical Greek authors, and is advancing into later Greek writing. The much smaller body of Old English Literature is also available. There are problems, however. Computer standardisation is relatively weak (as compared with tape recorders, say) and, as you have seen, the well-known corpora have used widely different methods of encoding their material, introducing idiosyncracy into each new project. A major effort, the *Text Encoding Initiative* is trying to get agreement on a consistent way of preparing corpora whether they are to be used in linguistic or literary research. Cutting across this, to some extent, is the fact that new computer media such as CD-ROM (Compact Disk Read-Only Memory) are being exploited commercially to make available dictionaries, encyclopedias and other information banks, many of which would be useful to linguists. A recent example is the version of the new Oxford edition of Shakespeare on CD-ROM. How to reconcile the use of this material (which often comes with a proprietary means of exploiting the data) with older media such as the combination of magnetic tape and disk used in general purpose computer installations is a problem. However, there can be no doubt that the means of investigating the resources of a language have been permanently transformed by the computer and corpora.

SUGGESTIONS FOR FURTHER READING

A most useful guide to several varieties of computer work with texts can be found in the Computers in Teaching Initiative Centre for Textual Studies *Resources Guide, March 1991*, edited by M. Deegan and S. Lee and obtainable from the CTI Centre for Textual Studies, Oxford University Computing Service, 13, Banbury Road, Oxford OX2 6NN. Much weightier is I. Lancashire (ed.) *The Humanities Computing Yearbook 1990* (Oxford, Clarendon Press, 1991) which is the standard reference work on all aspects of humanities computing, including text-processing, concordancing and corpora. Both of these give full details of the suppliers of the packages mentioned in the text.

There is as yet no introductory book-length treatment of corpus-based linguistics and research methods. John Sinclair's *Corpus, Concordance, Collocation* (Oxford University Press, 1991) describes the author's extensive work in using corpora as the basis for collocational and lexicographic research. Susan Hockey's *A Guide to Computer Applications in the Humanities* (London: Duckworth, 1980) covers a wide range, including text-processing languages and concordancing, but has not been updated to cover the enormous growth of recent years. Chris Butler's *Computers in Linguistics* (Oxford: Blackwell, 1985) covers some of the ground and gives a more palatable introduction to the SNOBOL4 programming language than the item cited in the text. B.H. Rudall and T. Corns *Computers and Literature: A Practical Guide* (Cambridge, Mass./Tunbridge

Wells: Abacus Press, 1987) assumes little knowledge of computing and discusses basic concepts in computing and the computer representation of textual material approachably.

In some ways it is easier to get the flavour of what corpus-based studies are about from reading conference papers, though they can sometimes be rather technical. A regular source of information is the *ICAME Journal* published annually by the International Computer Archive of Modern English and available from the Norwegian Computing Centre for the Humanities, PO Box 53, Universitet, N–5027 Bergen, Norway. ICAME acts as the distribution centre for many of the computer corpora of English and organises an annual conference. A good impression of what was going on in the late 1980s can be found in a set of papers edited by Willem Meijs, *Corpus Linguistics and Beyond: Proceedings of the 7th International Conference on English Language Research on Computer Corpora* (Amsterdam: Rodopi, 1987). R. Garside, G. Leech and G. Sampson have edited *The Computational Analysis of English: A Corpus-based Approach* (Harlow: Longman, 1987). Some of the papers are technical, but you will get a good idea of the problems which arose in producing the tagged version of the LOB corpus.

3   Speech Analysis and Recognition

PETER ROACH, DAVE MILLER and JOHN EMSLIE

When we look at how computers are used in speech laboratories we can see two different types of activity. In one, the computer serves as a tool in the way a microscope is a tool for a biologist or a telescope for an astronomer. In the other, we attempt to make use of the expert knowledge of the speech scientist in order to develop new ways of communicating with computers and handling information.

COMPUTER ANALYSIS OF SPEECH

Acoustic analysis

The most widespread application of computers in speech laboratories is for use as what we would like to call a speech microscope: the computer records a passage of speech in a way similar to a digital tape recorder and stores it. Once this information is recorded it can be played back as often as required; when we have recorded such speech data, we can say that we have captured a *speech signal*. Computer graphics is used to display the acoustic information, the most basic being the *waveform* representing the vibrations in the air that are picked up by the microphone; it is typical of many kinds of speech sound (the best example being vowels) that they show a clearly repeated pattern, as shown in Figure 1. The section of waveform that is repeated is called a *cycle* ; the rate of repetition per second of any part of the waveform is called its *frequency*, and that of the whole cycle is the *fundamental frequency*. Many other displays show the results of more complex analysis. One type is *filtering*, where energy in some parts of the frequency range is excluded and energy in others allowed to pass through. We can then measure the energy in a particular frequency range. It has long been known that a complex waveform can be broken down into a collection of simple waveforms called *sine waves*, in a way similar to the breaking of white light into

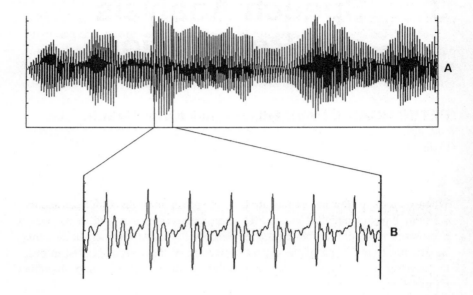

Figure 1: Waveform display of the sentence 'We rely on a railway' (A), and magnified view of part of the third syllable (B).

its component colours by a prism. It is mathematically difficult to analyse the *spectrum* of a sound in this way but computers using programs for what are called *Fast Fourier Transforms (FFTs)* can do the job for us very conveniently, allowing us to examine the *spectrum* of individual speech sounds. Mathematicians have also devised ways of analysing speech in a very efficient way called *Linear Predictive Coding (LPC)*. It would take too long to explain here how this works, but its greatest attraction is that it takes advantage of the predictability of speech waveforms – there is only a limited number of sounds that the human vocal tract can produce, and during the time that a sound of a particular type is being produced (e.g. a vowel, a nasal or a fricative) the sound will in general not vary in an unpredictable way. The result of the analysis is a set of numbers that represent the speech analysed: the computer is able to reconstitute the speech from the numbers by resynthesis so that you can listen to it to check that it sounds like the original, as a way of confirming that the analysis was correct.

An important capability for 'speech microscopes' is that of enabling the user to mark out a specific section of the recording for closer examination: usually two markers ('cursors') are moved by the user to chosen points on the computer screen along the time scale, and the computer will then display the selected portion in enlarged form. As well as looking, you can also listen repeatedly to this portion isolated from its context, and by rapid use of the cursors you can carry out a very efficient auditory and acoustic analysis of a passage; the visual display helps to guide the process. Of course, the 'speech microscope' is not limited to this routine application. Most systems are capable of a wide range of more sophisticated analyses and displays generated by programs like those described above. A very important one is the display of the 'pitch trace' (more properly called the fundamental frequency, or F0) corresponding to a selected portion of speech (Figure 2).

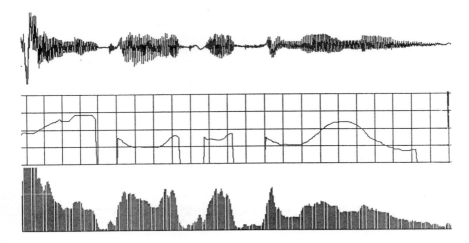

Figure 2: Display of the sentence 'Time and tide wait for no man'. Top: acoustic waveform; middle: "pitch trace" (fundamental frequency); bottom: intensity.

It is also possible to carry out a *spectral analysis* of a sound at a particular point in time. Looking at the spectra of different sounds enables detailed comparisons of quality to be made. In Figure 3 it is possible to see clear peaks at different points on the frequency scale, corresponding to the resonances that we call *formants*. These characterise different vowels. Sometimes it is more informative to have a display of speech in a sort of three-dimensional display (Figure 4) – such displays are sometimes called 'landscape' or 'waterfall' plots, and can be useful for emphasising aspects of the dynamic, continuously changing nature of speech. The type of spectral analysis and display most familiar to speech scientists is the *spectrogram*, which is the most difficult and time-consuming to produce on a computer (Figure 5).

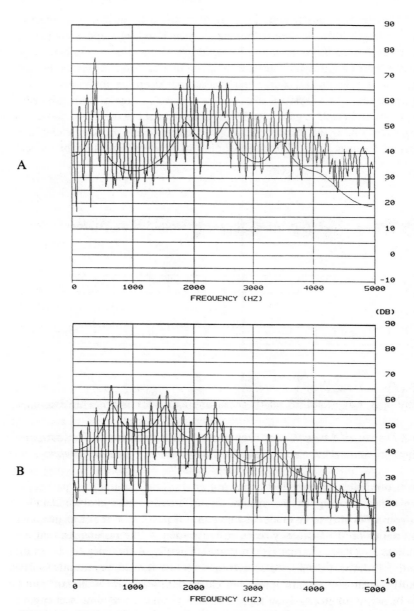

Figure 3: Acoustic spectra of two different vowels. (A) the vowel in 'bit', showing major peaks at around 375, 1800, 2550 and 3400 Hz; (B) the vowel in 'bat', with peaks at 600, 1500, 2350 and 3315 Hz.

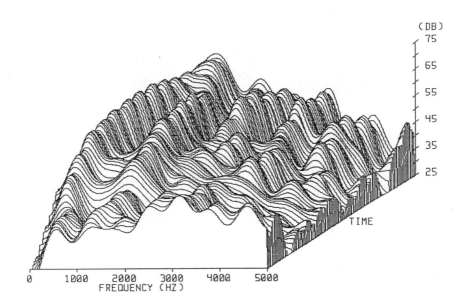

Figure 4: 'Waterfall' or 'landscape' display of the word 'John' /dʒɒn/.

What sorts of application are 'speech microscopes' put to? On the research side they are obviously useful for making measurements: for example, in examining speech rhythm it is very easy to measure the interval between one stressed syllable and another (as long as you know where you want the starting and ending points for your measurements to be): Figure 6 shows a very simple example – the sentence 'Take time today to do the dishes' with the durations of the inter-stress intervals marked.

In studying the way we use the pitch of the voice in speech, we might look at the fundamental frequency of an utterance in order to measure the frequency of the highest point of the pitch movement; in the case of a "tone language' such as Chinese we might look at the fundamental frequency of the different tones that serve to distinguish different word meanings in that language. In addition to these applications, samples of speech that are felt to be particularly important can be stored by the computer to form part of a research archive or database that can be re-examined at a later date. There are also obvious teaching applications. The ability to select and replay makes it possible to bring a particular pronunciation problem to a language student's attention very effectively, and the production of

Figure 5: Spectrogram of the sentence 'We rely on a railway'.

tape-recorded teaching material using edited extracts from recordings of natural speech is made much easier and more efficient than conventional tape-editing. In the case of teaching the deaf or those with speech handicaps it is possible for the teacher or therapist to use a computer display of speech information to help the pupil to improve the intelligibility of their speech.

All the above illustrations refer to the processing and display of acoustic information – the information that can be found in the sound wave. Sometimes it is more informative to examine or display some aspect of the way speech is *produced,* and this sort of analysis is described in the next section.

Analysis of speech production

Speech, to the phonetics researcher, is more than just sound. To understand this, we need to refer, briefly and in general terms, to the way the speech we hear is produced. This is done in more detail in Chapter 5. The great majority of the speech sounds used in the world's languages are initiated by much the same kind of muscular activity as that controlling our breathing. An *airstream* produced by an increase of pressure inside the lungs is acted upon by the speech organs of the vocal system to create a number of *sound sources.* One example of a sound source is the series of air pulses into which the airstream is broken by the vibrating vocal folds. This is the source of the *voice* and the basis of vowels and similar sounds. Another quite different source is the air turbulence produced when the airflow passes through a narrow constriction in the mouth, for example when the tongue is held quite close to the roof of the mouth, causing the hissing noise of the initial sounds in 'sip' and 'ship'. The physical result of all the activity of speech production is that the pressure and volume of the airstream are modified; the airstream moves out of the throat, mouth and nose (which make up the *vocal tract*); pressure changes in the surrounding air result, and the *sound pressure* wave is radiated. This is the sound which we hear and which is picked up by the microphone.

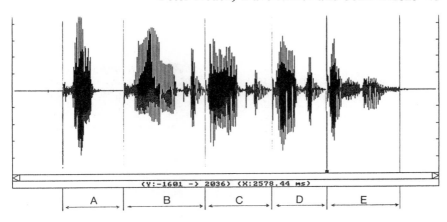

Figure 6: Measurement of the time intervals between stressed syllable onsets in 'Take time today to do the dishes'.

It follows from what we have just said that there are a number of places we can go for information about the nature of a speech sound wave. For some purposes, the airstream itself is of interest and it is possible to collect the airflow emerging from the lips or the nostrils using a special mask containing electronic *transducers* which convert the airflow into an electrical signal that can be fed into the computer for analysis. The amount of air *pressure* above and below the vocal folds can also be very valuable information: a thin pressure tube placed in the mouth or the throat can provide this, again converted into an electrical signal.

Other signals are of interest in speech and are often processed by computer. An important field of study is to try to explain how the dimensions of the vocal tract are altered by movements of the jaw, tongue, lips and soft palate, and to find out exactly how these organs behave. Many instrumental techniques – too many to describe in full here – have been devised for experimental work of this type, and we will look at a few. One that has become quite popular is *electropalatography*, an electronic technique for detecting contact between the tongue and the palate; an artificial palate similar to a plate used for dentures is made to fit a particular speaker, and contains over sixty tiny electrodes. When the tongue touches any electrode, this event and its position is detected electronically and fed to a computer. This information can later be analysed like a film in slow motion, with synchronised sound-track. Figure 7 shows an EPG record[7] of the consonant

---

[7] Reproduced from W.J. Hardcastle and P.J. Roach, 'Instrumental investigation of coarticulation in stop consonant sequences', in H.H. and P. Hollien (eds), *Current Issues in the Phonetic Sciences*. Amsterdam: John Benjamins, 1979, pp. 531–540.

```
                            Alveolar closure
      342              343        ↓ 344           345              346
00......00    00......00    00......00    00....000   000....000
00....00      00....00      00....00      00....00    0000.000
0......0      0......0      00....00      00....00    00....00
........      .......0      0......0      0.....00    00....00
........      ........      0......0      0......0    00....00
........      ........      00000000      00000000    00000000
......        ......        .00.0.        000000      000000
```

```
                                          Velar closure  Alveolar release
      347              348          349        ↓ 350           ↓ 351
00000..000   00000.0000   00000.0000   0000000000   0000000000
0000.000     0000.000     0000.000     0000.000     0000.000
00....00     00....00     00....00     00....00     00...000
00....00     00....00     00....00     00....00     00....00
00...000     00....00     00....00     00....00     00...000
00000000     0000.000     00...000     00....00     00....00
00000000     00000000     00000000     00...000     00....00
000000       000000       000000       000000       00...0
```

```
      352              353          354           355              356
0000000000   00000.0000   0000000000   0000000000   0000000000
0000.000     0000.000     0000.000     0000.000     0000.000
000..000     000..000     000..000     000..000     000..000
00...000     000..000     000..000     00...000     00...000
000..000     000..000     000..000     00...000     00.,..00
0000..00     0000..00     00....00     00....00     .0....00
000....0     0......0     0......0     0......0     .......0
0.....       0.....       ......       ......       ......
```

```
                  Velar release
      357        ↓ 358          359           360              361
0000000000   00000.0000   00000.0000   00000.0000   000...000
0000.000     0000.000     0000.000     0000.000     0000.000
000..000     000..000     000..000     00...000     00....00
00...000     000.0000     00....00     00....00     00....00
00....00     00....00     00....00     0.....00     00....00
.......0     .......0     .......0     ......00     0......0
........     ........     ........     ........     ........
......       ......       ......       ......       ......
```

```
      362              363          364           365              366
000....000   00.....000   00......00   00......00   00......00
0000.000     0000.000     0000.000     0000.000     0000.000
00....00     00....00     00....00     00....00     00...000
00....00     00....00     00....00     00....00     00....00
0......0     0......0     0......0     0......0     0......0
........     ........     ........     ........     ........
........     ........     ........     ........     ........
......       ......       ......       ......       ......
```

Figure 7: Printout of electropalatographic data from /æ/ to /t/ in 'catkin'.

cluster /tk/ in the middle of the word 'catkin'. Each numbered frame shows the state of tongue-palate contact at intervals of one-hundredth of a second. The top of each frame represents the velar region (where the back of the tongue touches for /k/ and /g/) and the lower part represents the alveolar region (just behind the upper front teeth). A small dot indicates no contact, while a large circle (O) indicates contact. If you read through the frames one by one you will see that there is a period of overlap when there is both an alveolar closure /t/ and a velar one /k/ at the same time, though the /t/ begins first and the /k/ ends last. Such records, particularly when combined with data from other instruments, can be very valuable in investigating how speech is produced.

A very difficult and advanced instrumental technique is *electromyography*, in which the tiny electrical signals given off by muscle fibres when they contract are detected by implanted wires. One vital function for the computer here is to extract the very weak signal from amongst a lot of 'background noise' by special signal processing. X-rays have played a very important part in the development of instrumental studies of speech, but we have become so conscious of the dangers associated with radiation that this technique has become much less widely used. However, a new computerised X-ray system has begun to change this situation. A tiny beam of radiation is moved with pin-point accuracy across a small area where marker points have been fixed on articulators such as the tongue and lips, being switched on for only a brief exposure to enable the computer to locate the markers. The technique is complicated and expensive, but much safer than conventional X-ray equipment. The information is recorded on a computer so that it can be analysed and compared.

One of the most challenging areas in speech research is the activity of the larynx during speech. Much of the work on this has been carried out by means of optical instruments such as laryngoscopic mirrors and high-speed cine-cameras, but a number of other techniques give us an accurate, if indirect, view of what we want to see. We will look at how we can combine information from different sources to build up a picture of the nature of vocal fold vibration. We have already mentioned the possibility of recording airflow from the speaker's mouth; in addition to this we can record the opening and closing of the vocal folds during voicing by using a device called a *laryngograph*, or *electroglottograph*, which works by passing a very weak alternating current between two electrodes on the outside of the throat and detecting the changes in electrical impedance as the folds open and close. We can also add to this information the microphone signal. All of these signals exist in the form of electrical *analogs* (or copies) of the activity that is being recorded, but to use them in the computer we must convert them into *digital* form (i.e. into numbers). This is done by a piece of computer equipment called an *analog-to-digital converter*, or *A-to-D converter*.

The practical use of a computer to analyse speech production can be illustrated from a piece of research in progress in our laboratory. The physiological system that produces voice is capable of working in several different ways, and it is thought that significant variations in the sound wave may result. To help in the study of this, aerodynamic as well as acoustic signals are recorded. The apparatus used includes a microphone, to record the sound pressure wave, another transducer attached to a face-mask, to record the pattern of airflow coming out of the mouth, and a laryngograph whose principal function in this case is to indicate the timing of successive vocal fold vibrations, because the analysis method used requires the signals to be broken up on this basis. Air pressure in the mouth is also recorded, but for present purposes this signal need not be discussed. All the channels of data are read by the computer at the same time and converted into digital form.

When a pulse of air is released by the vibrating vocal folds it causes a change in air pressure, and the resulting pressure wave is modified by the particular shape of the vocal tract. The first step in this research is to try to find out as much as possible about that air pulse and its general relationship to the air supply the speaker is using. This can tell us quite a lot about the efficiency with which the voice is functioning, as well as the strength of the resulting speech pressure wave. The next step is to try to get a more detailed picture of the shape of the pulse, since this can have significant effects on the corresponding spectrum.

The important and technically difficult job that the computer must do for us in this research, therefore, is to work backwards from the acoustic and airflow signals to the original simpler wave pattern coming from the larynx. Figure 8 shows, firstly, the airflow waveform (A) of an /e/ vowel (as in 'pen'), picked up by the transducer in the face-mask. Since we only use this for fairly general information it simplifies our job if this signal is filtered to remove most of the higher frequencies, producing the waveform shown as B. Next, an interactive computer program allows us to remove other effects of the vocal tract to produce something close to the original series of pulses from the larynx (C). This is a process known as *inverse filtering*, not to be confused with the more routine operation of filtering that has already been introduced. We have used microphone signals, like the one displayed as D in the figure, to study pulse shapes, again by using the inverse filtering process. The program requires not only the speech wave as input, but also the laryngograph signal and a timing signal derived from it by a separate program. These are used to work out how much of the total duration of each cycle is to be analysed. The resulting waveform can be displayed. A single cycle is shown as E in Figure 8. We can think of this as a single flow-pulse, if we remember that it is in fact only *evidence* of that pulse (since we derived it from speech pressure – the microphone signal – and not the airflow that gives rise to

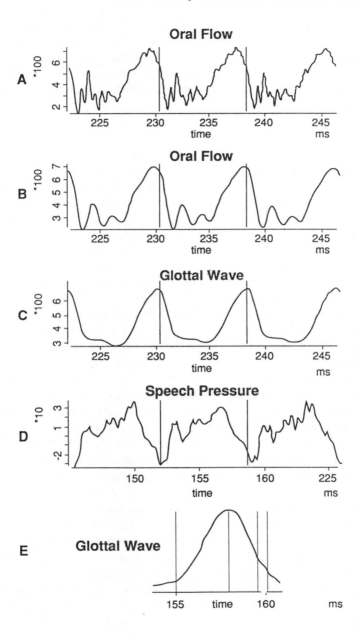

Figure 8: Airflow and acoustic waveforms of vocal fold vibration.

pressure changes). In this case the relatively smooth, symmetrical shape is consistent with a voice that is rather breathy in quality. The vertical lines drawn on the graph show some of the kinds of measurement usually taken from the time axis, and it can be seen that intervals smaller than one thousandth of a second are involved. Such detail is clearly impossible without digital sampling and computer graphics.

SPEECH RECOGNITION BY COMPUTER

One of the most interesting developments in the computing world (from our point of view) is the development of the technology to enable computers to recognise what is said to them: speech science and traditional phonetics have a very valuable role to play in this area. Looking a few years into the future, it is expected that you will be able to dictate a letter or a report into a microphone, and the computer will print out the document for you – correctly spelled and punctuated, of course. This may be quite useful to us, but will be considerably more useful in societies where typing is difficult or impossible, such as those with highly complex writing systems (Chinese, Japanese), and those with widespread illiteracy. Those who will benefit most will be disabled people who do not have the hand control necessary for typing. In the more immediate term, the technology already exists for computer recognition of vocabularies of hundreds or even thousands of spoken words, and although the commercial world is being very cautious about taking up this innovation, there is a growing number of application areas where information is being given to computers via speech. The most promising areas are those where computers are needed but the users have their hands and/or eyes busy. For example, the pilot of an aircraft might want to request some complex information from an on-board computer about the plane's condition, a surgeon might want to request information about a patient's past treatment while carrying out an operation, and a surveyor for a motorway construction project or an archaeologist might want to record measurements they are making while standing ankle-deep in mud. Speech recognition is already being used experimentally for such applications, as well as in more mundane tasks such as airport baggage-handling, map-making, in-car telephone dialling, warehouse inventory checking and telephone enquiries to computer information systems such as banking services and travel timetables. And again, the disabled can benefit in many ways such as by being able to control all their domestic appliances (e.g. heating, television, telephone and door-locks) by the spoken word.

How does automatic speech recognition work, and how can work in our subject help? We will start by looking at one way of tackling the simplest sort of recognition, that which recognises individual words one at a time, separated by pauses. If you look again at the spectrogram in Figure 5 (which was produced by a small computer), you can see that the visible pattern is made up of different levels of grey (between almost black and completely white). Imagine laying a transparent sheet of squared paper over this and writing in each square a number indicating how black that square is (say, 10 for completely black and 1 for white). At the end of that process (which the computer could carry out in a fraction of a second) you would have a sheet of graph paper with a two-dimensional grid of numbers on it. Imagine that we construct one of these patterns (or *templates*) for each of ten words or phrases: when the computer has these patterns stored in its memory, any word spoken into the microphone can be analysed in the same way and compared square by square with each of the ten stored patterns, and the stored pattern that shows the biggest number of similarities will be chosen by the computer to be its best guess as to what the user said to it. This is a very simplified account of the sort of technique used; many technical problems have had to be overcome before the template-matching approach worked well enough to be put into commercial systems. For example, a way had to be found of compensating for the fact that we might say a word more rapidly in everyday speaking than we did in the initial 'training' stage, or that our voice might change as we get tired after several hours of work. At the moment, almost all such systems have to be 'trained' separately for each speaker who will be using it – they are not good at adapting to differences between speakers, and are usually described as 'speaker-dependent'.

At the level of isolated-word recognition, speech science does not have a great deal to contribute. However, it has long been accepted that the isolated-word recognition approach will not be adequate for the long-term goal of *large-vocabulary, speaker-independent, connected-speech* recognition – computers simply cannot do word template matching on the tens of thousands of words that we use in everyday language. Apart from the difficulty of dealing with the large number of word templates, there is the problem that in connected speech each word is likely to appear in a large variety of forms according to whether or not the word receives stress, according to context and according to how fast the speaker is speaking. Consider how the word 'that' will be pronounced in the following examples:

1. I want *that* one.
2. How much is that doggy in the window?
3. That he was guilty was beyond question.
4. I hope that it'll be all right.

Even more extreme variability is found in the word 'and', which ranges from a fully pronounced, stressed version to a brief /n/ sound in 'fish and chips'. No word has a fixed, unvarying pronunciation, so each word template would have to be supplied with a number of permitted alternative versions. The preferred alternative to recognising whole words is to look for smaller (*sub-word*) units: at the lowest level, we can try to recognise the individual speech sounds, so that for recognising the name 'Sam' we would have to train the computer to recognise /s/, /æ/ and /m/. Of course, these sounds (known as *phonemes*) are themselves liable to vary in context, but since there are only thirty or forty of them in English it is not nearly such a lengthy job to work out the ways in which they vary, though the techniques used for recognition are usually a lot more complex than the simple example given for word template-matching above. Many researchers have concluded that the phoneme is too small a unit to work with, and that variability is easier to deal with if we look at slightly larger units: one that has been tried is the *diphone* (a pair of adjacent phonemes); another is the *syllable*, which is often claimed to be a basic and universal unit in all human languages. English has about 10,000 different syllables, however, so an easier alternative is to divide syllables into half (*demisyllables*) and try to recognise beginnings and ends of syllables separately instead. Several ingenious combinations of approach have been tried. Whichever sub-word unit is used, an essential stage in the recognition process is to have a dictionary in the computer's memory that lists all the words of the language in the form of the sounds they are made of. For example, if the machine has recognised the phonemes /trɒf/, the dictionary search will turn up the word spelt 'trough'. Often the search will turn up several alternatives. For example, the phoneme sequence /beə/ will produce at least 'bear' (noun), 'bear' (verb), 'bare' (verb) and 'bare' (adjective); the computer will be able to decide between these options only by taking into account the context in which the word is encountered and the contexts in which it usually occurs (so that, for example, the context 'I can't ... it' will rule out the noun and adjective possibilities, and the expression 'I can't bear/bare it' hardly ever occurs with the second verb possibility), so some sophisticated linguistic knowledge has to be built into the computer system. Of course, the computer would be unable to distinguish the different meanings without the context, but then so would you be.

Clearly, the kind of analysis involved in recognising sub-word units needs a lot of knowledge about human speech and about the particular language being recognised. The computer needs to know the different variants of the units being recognised, the way they behave in different linguistic contexts, the range of possible combinations the units are found in and their relative frequency of occurrence. Future recognition systems will also make use of speech information that is currently little used, such as stress, rhythm and intonation. Work in speech laboratories is contributing valuable information to the development of these advanced speech recognition systems, and a great deal of basic research on speech remains to be done.

SUGGESTIONS FOR FURTHER READING

The best introduction to the basics of speech acoustics is S. Rosen and P. Howell, *Signals and Systems for Speech and Hearing* (London: Academic Press, 1991). As an alternative, you could read D.B. Fry, *The Physics of Speech* (Cambridge University Press, 1979). Most of the techniques for measuring aspects of speech production are outlined in G. Borden and K. Harris *A Speech Science Primer* (Baltimore: Williams and Wilkins, 2nd edn, 1984), though not much has been written about computer techniques for processing such data.

Most books and papers describing computer speech recognition tend to be difficult for readers whose maths and physics are limited. The treatment by J. Vaissière in F. Fallside and W.A. Woods *Computer Speech Processing* (London: Prentice Hall, 1985) is clear and straightforward. The best books are W.A. Ainsworth *Speech Recognition by Machine* (London: Peter Peregrinus, 1988) and J.N. Holmes *Speech Synthesis and Recognition* (London: van Nostrand Reinhold, 1988).

4 Processing Natural Language

TIM WILLIS

How can we tell a computer to do something, or ask it a question in plain English? This chapter will explain the basics of 'natural language processing' – what it is, how it is done, and how it can be used. There are various times when it is useful to be able to command a computer in plain English, or interrogate it for information. In order to act upon human input the computer must be able to take it apart and form a logical representation of what it is fundamentally saying – it must to some degree 'understand' the input. Likewise, when it has an answer, it must be able to express its abstract representation of the knowledge in a way comprehensible to a human operator, by 'generating' natural language. This is not as simple in practice as might at first appear. Human language is full of ambiguities, words and phrases that can mean several different things, shortened forms of words and sentences, and other factors that can serve to cloud meaning. Think how often you have to ask someone to express something another way, or re-read a sentence. If we cannot understand each other all the time, it would be unrealistic to expect a computer to outperform us in our own medium.

There are many possible applications of language-recognition and generation systems, in the home, in the workplace, in schools and colleges, libraries, and transport. The largest is the fast and simple recovery of information from a database, in an easy-to-understand form. Many people are constrained by not knowing the computer language needed to instruct one to, for example, search out all the information on a specific subject like a historical character and arrange it by date. Getting to know a new system can be infuriating, especially where one makes a mistake and has to follow the wrong path for several steps in order to start again. It would be far simpler and more efficient to be able to hold a conversation with the machine, in which the user specified what they wanted, and the computer asked for clarification of any details. The possible uses are endless – anything that could be built into a database of knowledge, from train times and routes, to lists of drug properties and side-effects for pharmacists and doctors, or even the entire contents of an encyclopedia, could be rapidly gleaned by the computer for the required information. And this database could be updated and amended instantly. With an electronic network one could access one database (of a particular field) from anywhere in the country. An extension of this is that a computer which could communicate in our language could be a portable, personal tutor, adapting precisely to the needs of the individual pupil. The method of 'interrogation' could be via a keyboard, or spoken. The latter is a lot more difficult to achieve, and at the time of writing, we know of no system that can cope with more than a limited vocabulary.

The way in which the input language is disassembled into abstract units of meaning for analysis, and reconstructed for its answer, lends itself to the process of machine translation. Since the input is broken down into a supposedly language-neutral form, it should in theory be fairly straightforward to re-express it in a different human language, provided all the rules are fed in.

Computer language processing (see Chapter 3) can also provide many disabled people with more independence and privacy, enabling them to control televisions, telephones and other appliances from a keyboard or by voice, in English. If and when we develop robots for the home, these will be particularly useful for physically disabled people, and will need to produce and understand language. There are already machines that will read out loud newspapers, books and typewritten letters for visually-impaired people, attempting a correct pronunciation and intonation. Work is being done on analysis of handwritten text and on voice-driven word-processors to type out speech. Machines with vocabularies of around 10,000 words are expected soon to be available. These have to be trained for each speaker. Both types of machine need an extensive knowledge of natural language for several reasons – to help them with areas where the language becomes difficult to read or hear, to help produce correct intonation if reading it, and to be able to distinguish the right pronunciation where there is a choice, as in the case of 'lead' or 'bow'. Sometimes a word's position in the sentence will rule out one interpretation; in 'I lead the way', 'lead' can only be the verb, but in 'It's in the lead' we need a larger context to work out which noun is intended. A speech-to-text system – a word processor you can speak to – also needs to be able to tell first what the probable division of the sentence into words is, involving a degree of trial and error. As with the spellcheckers built into some word-processors, it will need to ask the speaker to verify some of its decisions as to whether there is a mistake or just a word or construction new to it. A computer can be used to teach a language, foreign or one's own, by demonstrating and correcting its use.

One common leisure implementation of natural language production and analysis is the computer adventure, in which the player controls the actions of an alter-ego within the game, asking it to perform tasks and give feedback. Anyone with some knowledge of a programming language like BASIC can write a simple program to take apart or generate sentences, and quite quickly a semblance of understanding may be produced. However, these can be tripped up as soon as something too complicated is typed in – even if they attempt a defence like 'I don't understand you'. An eventual goal of computer science is to produce an artificial mind that won't trip up like this, and will hold its own against a human mind – an artificial intelligence. The Turing test, devised by the mathematician Alan Turing, is designed to verify whether this can be done. His idea was to pit a human 'interrogator' against two subjects one human, the other a computer communicating from different rooms by teletype (or computer screen nowadays). Each tries to convince a succession of interrogators that *it* is the human. If, after a number of tests, the computer convinces its interrogators 50% of the time that it is the human, it has passed the test. As yet, machines that pass the test still only exist in science fiction, although work involving 'neural networks' and parallel processing looks promising.

THE STRUCTURE OF ENGLISH

One way of setting about programming a computer for the tasks of producing and analysing English would be the 'brute force' approach, in which the computer would simply be fed as many of the possible sentences in English as possible. This is a very inefficient way of doing things for several reasons, among them the vast amount of memory it would take up and the time involved in trying to match an input systematically against hundreds of thousands of sentences, many of them similar in all but a couple of words. Fortunately, there are discernible structures within the English language that enable most of the possible sentences in it to be 'boiled down' into a much reduced form.

Traditional grammar textbooks found in schools tend to set out the formal side of a language, corresponding to the perceived ideals of how the author feels it *should* be used rather than to how it actually is in practice. Hence examples are somewhat concocted (and indeed can become amusing after some years – some genuine phrases from one grammar book include '"You are Miss A, I am sure" – "You are under a strange delusion, I am Mrs C."' and 'You are looking very pale about the gills. I hope, you are not going to feed the fishes.'). 'Real life' language is full of colloquialisms, with whole chunks missed out, and deviations from standard grammar. This might be because we wish to express our individuality, emphasise a point or avoid repetition. We use various ways of speeding up our communication, such as compacting our language: either dropping whole phrases that have already been stated once (elision) or substituting shorter paraphrases or pronouns for information already expressed. An example of elision would be replying to 'Who is in charge here?' with 'I am' rather than 'I am <in charge here>.' A speaker or writer will often use unconventional language for novelty, by mistake or through ignorance. Programming a computer to process a restricted set of 'perfect' language is a great deal easier than getting one to deal with the real thing. We will start by examining how a restricted set of 'grammatically correct' sentences can be analysed or produced, before moving on to the less sure-footed area of full, unedited natural language.

For the purposes of this chapter, a 'text' is a piece of language which is represented in written, machine-readable and human-readable form, such as this chapter itself. We will not in this chapter confront the issues involved in converting a speech waveform into a representation of 'words' and 'sentences', nor delve into the possibilities of processing sign language by computer.

When a person wishes to express a thought by producing a sentence, it will involve a number of concepts. Some may be clear from previous utterances, and others may need prominence as 'new' information. The linguist and psychologist Noam Chomsky believed that underlying the 'surface structure' of written or spoken language (i.e. its form as we perceive it) there is a 'deep' level representing our actual thoughts, which is independent of any specific language. These are then shaped by the specific rules of the language they are to be expressed in, and further re-ordered and adjusted to bring forward some elements for emphasis. The result is the 'surface structure' or 'realisation' (the actual sentence produced). Thus, a simple message about the action of an apple (the 'patient'), being given by one person (John, the 'actor') to another (Mary, the 'recipient') can be expressed in many different ways. Some possible realizations could be:

1. John gave the apple to Mary.
2. John gave Mary the apple.
3. The apple was given (to) Mary by John.
4. The apple was given by John to Mary.
5. Mary was given the apple by John.
6. *Mary was given by John the apple.
7. John, who is a friend of mine, gave the apple to Mary.
8. John quickly gave the apple to Mary.

The first sentence is the neutral, 'unmarked' word order. In the second there is a slight difference which might be used to make a more varied style within a text. In 3 and 4, the patient is 'fronted' into the most noticeable position in the sentence, necessitating the more complex passive construction around the verb.

In the fifth, and grammatically unacceptable sixth sentences, it is the recipient that is emphasised, again resulting in a more complex expression of the verb. Some linguists refer to the items fitting the above semantic roles of 'actor', 'patient' and 'recipient' as being the 'underlying subject', 'underlying direct object' and 'underlying indirect object', respectively.

Oddly, not all combinations are permissible. What is so strange about sentence 6 as to make it unacceptable grammatically, when we can still see what it is saying? (Ungrammatical sentences are conventionally prefixed with an asterisk, questionable ones with a question mark.) Number 7 is a variation with the same word order as 1, only with additional information inserted about the subject. In 8 the verb is qualified with an indication of 'how' it was done. Each of the first five sentences gives a different emphasis to the items John, Mary and the apple, but we would agree that the relationship between the three items is preserved throughout. *Parsing* is the term for the process by which the sentence is dissected in order to reconstruct the underlying thought, noting other information conveyed by word order, elision and anything else expressed covertly, conveying information not actually in the words themselves. The outward representation of the sentence (its surface structure) is broken down into an abstract, representational framework of its underlying (deep) structure. This is then more conducive to further processing, working out the purpose of the sentence, such as asking a question or making a statement. Before we examine some of the basic processes of parsing, we must look at how sentences are put together.

Phrase structure grammar

As the examples showed, a sentence is made up of a number of distinct constituent parts, each of which can be expanded upon, and each of which can be moved around as a unit, within the sentence, subject to various restrictions. These can be given various labels or 'phrase markers', which are conventionally written in capital letters. For our purposes we will begin with the assumption that every sentence contains a verb, and push to one side examples like 'Out of sight, out of mind'. We will also deal only with one-clause sentences. The verb phrase (VP) is the part of the sentence describing the action or relationship, and may be several words long, depending on the tense (past, present, future or combinations such as 'will have had'), mood (statement, question, exclamation or command) and voice (active or passive). Some grammarians include everything bar the subject within the 'VP'. Sentences in the first three moods will always contain at least one noun phrase (NP), the subject of the action. We will leave for the moment imperatives like 'Go away!', which make up a fairly small percentage of everyday usage. At its simplest, then, a sentence pattern 'S' consists of a noun phrase and a verb phrase, each of which can be minimally expressed with one word. For example:

9. Doves fly.

The reason for calling an NP or VP a phrase, even when it only consists of one word, is its similarity grammatically to groups of several words. For consistency, we add the more expansive category to the description of the sentence.

This pattern can be represented with a sort of linguistic algebra thus:

(i) S → NP + VP

where the arrow means 'the item on the left can broken down into the item(s) on the right' or, 'the items on the right when put together generate the item on the left'. Expansion of the rules leads to a basic framework both for generating sentences and analysing them (taking them apart). The set of rules constitutes a *generative phrase structure grammar*. The grammar is very conducive to being implemented in an algorithm or program.

The NP can also contain a determiner ('the', 'a', 'my', 'some', etc.) and/or one or more adjectives.

10. [The beautiful white doves] fly.

We can therefore add other rules to the above, this time breaking down the potential structure of NPs:

   (ii) NP → noun
  (iii) NP → det + noun
  (iv) NP → adj + noun
   (v) NP → det + adj + noun
  (vi) NP → det + adj + adj + noun

and so on. What makes structures like this particularly suited to computing is the way the above rules can be reduced to one 'catch-all' formula. Firstly, adjectives can, theoretically, be added *ad infinitum*, and this is represented in the formula by an asterisk meaning 'as many times as you like'. Thus (v) and (vi) can be collapsed into a single rule

  (vii) NP → det + adj* + noun

By enclosing in 'curly' brackets any items which are optional, rules (ii) to (vii) can be expressed as

(viii)   NP → {det} + {adj*} + noun

In the formulae, an expression in lower case means 'this can be replaced with any word in the language from this word class'. Hence at the moment our rule allows noun phrases like 'seagulls', 'the blue whales', 'my sleek fast red convertible sports car', not to mention some undesirables like *'a cliffs', and *'many dead table'. Note that here we are talking about grammatical acceptability – that is, the rules about the permissible ordering of words and groups of words. Thus the real-world consideration that inanimate objects cannot properly be described as dead because they never lived is irrelevant here. The last phrase is only grammatically unacceptable because of the lack of number agreement between the determiner and the noun. We leave questions of meaning until later.

The verb phrase can also be expanded, and these expansions formularised. It may include an auxiliary, like 'will', 'can', 'have', 'do', as in:

11. Your father will hit the roof.

If the verb is transitive, a second NP can be added after the VP, thus:

12. The car hit the wall.

and if it is ditransitive, two NPs:

13. Mary sold John her car.

(ix)   VP → {aux} + verb + {NP} + {NP}

A prepositional phrase (PP) is made up of a preposition and an NP, thus:

(x)   PP → prep + NP

PPs can be added to an NP to give added information about the 'thing', or to a VP to qualify some detail about the event, such as its location, time or manner in which it happened; there is no theoretical limit to their number:

14. The bird with the white tail flew in a flash onto the tree with the apples.

Adding PPs to the rules for describing NPs and VPs, we get:

(xi) NP → NP + {PP}
(xii) VP → VP + {PP}

After a moment's consideration two things become clear:

(a) The phrase labels have invoked themselves on the right-hand side.
(b) The NP and PP patterns can invoke each other.

This potential for circularity is called *recursiveness*. It is this property that enables the small set of eventual rules evolved here to describe the structure of, or generate, a very large number of the possible sentences of English. As they stand, however, they are too powerful since we have not yet imposed restrictions on which members of each word class can combine in the same sentence. The set of rules expressed above form a 'context-free grammar'. Nor have we yet addressed the problems of semantics – the description of meaning.

This approach to making or chopping up phrases and sentences can be seen in so-called slot-and-filler exercises in foreign language learning textbooks, where a sequence can be constructed by picking an item from each box moving left to right. Some boxes may stretch across a space where two or more choices can be combined as an alternative. As an example in English, an NP can consist of a determiner, adjective and noun added together, or alternatively one word – a pronoun like 'I', or a proper noun like 'Jenny'. This method can easily be implemented on a computer, in BASIC for instance. We can also list words in a computerised dictionary, complete with information about their grammatical category, number and person. There are various ways of speeding up a lookup mechanism to give all the relevant data on any particular word.

TREE STRUCTURES

A common way of representing the hierarchical nature of sentence and phrase formation graphically is the 'tree structure' (Figure 1a). Rather confusingly, the 'tree' is upside-down and would better be described as a 'root' system, but nonetheless it shows how the units of different size fit together.

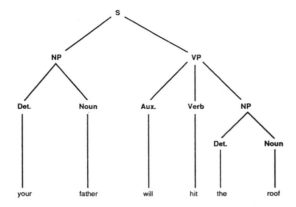

Figure 1a: A sample tree structure.

The grammar above can produce two different tree structures for a sentence like

15. Nancy cleaned the board with the blue cloth.

There is a difference between what the two are actually saying. In Figure 1b, the context involves a board being wiped with the cloth in question; in Figure 1c, the board is one covered in blue cloth, like a display pin-board, and the instrument for cleaning it is unspecified. Only the context will make the meaning clear, and sometimes it is simply impossible to resolve an ambiguity with certainty.

Context free grammars can generate or show the simple structure of a sentence, but they do not show *why* each constituent is where it is in the sentence. To describe the *function* of each constituent (such as 'underlying subject', 'time phrase' etc.), more complicated systems are needed.

Transition networks

It is possible to illustrate the processes involved in generating or analysing a sentence, using a 'map' of the stages gone through. The most basic of these is a transition network, which consists of 'states' reached in the generation/analysis, represented as lettered circular islands on the diagram, and 'transitions', represented by arcs between them (Figure 2). The arcs are one-way, and arrowed to show direction. Numbering them also helps, as they can be referred to as NP3 and so on. Whether generating or analysing NPs, the process involves 'matching' a word at a time to the word class label of the next available arc, and crossing it

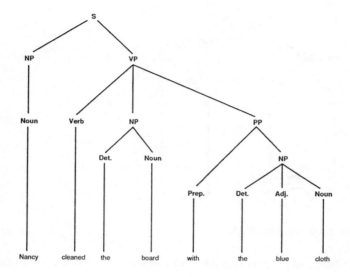

Figure 1b: Ambiguous sentence, first analysis.

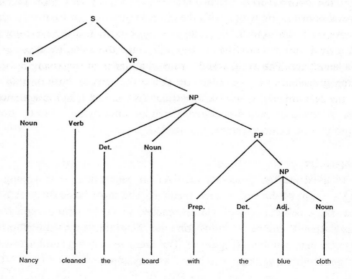

Figure 1c: Ambiguous sentence, second analysis.

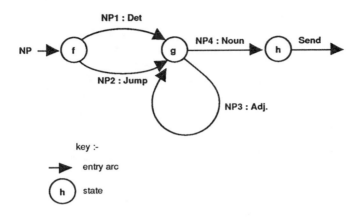

Figure 2: NP network.

to the next state. This is something like trying to fit a string of different shaped blocks across a network of corresponding holes. We need a 'lookup' subroutine to give the current word's class. Some networks may have arcs that represent other, smaller networks, in which case one matches a phrase rather than a word (briefly glance ahead at Figure 4). The process starts at an Initial State, marked with a small arrow (in the network in Figure 2, 'f') and ends by leaving the network on a 'send' arc. The arc marked 'jump' is a means of bypassing optional items, and simply means you do not have to tick off or add an item on this arc. To generate the NP 'my big saggy old beanbag' you would follow the network thus:

my	big	saggy	old	beanbag	
arc NP1	arc NP3	arc NP3	arc NP3	arc NP4	**SEND**

f>>determiner>>g g>>adjective>>g g>>adjective>>g g>>adjective>>g g>>noun>>h

To generate the one-word NP 'doves', you would take the jump arc NP2 from (f) to (g), followed by the noun arc NP4 from (g) to (h). The function performed if using the network to analyse a sequence that already exists is called 'recognising' it – somewhat analogous to 'recognising' a nation, and giving it your stamp of approval. If a sequence that does not fit is fed into the network, like 'the my house', the process fails to match the NP to its pattern of an acceptable one, in this instance stopping at state (g), and unable to find an arc to match the second determiner against. It does not necessarily mean the sequence is wrong yet, just that the network as it stands cannot accept it.

This network can be improved upon to take into account prepositional phrases (PPs) within NPs, as in 'the door [of the garage]', 'the fish [in the water]', and pronouns and proper nouns. The phrases inside square brackets will each traverse arc NP7 (Figure 3). It is at this stage that the circularity concept crops up again.

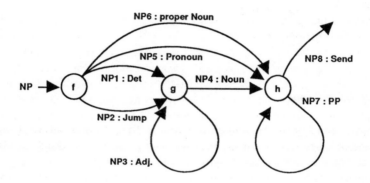

Figure 3: Improved NP network.

To define a PP, we do so in terms of a preposition and an NP added together. If we draw up a network for PPs, and label the second arc not with a word class, but the name of another arc, we condense the whole NP network in this map to a single representative arc PP2 (Figure 4). The one line on the PP network labelled NP, then, refers to the NP process, and the one labelled PP in the noun phrase network to the whole PP network. The networks are now called recursive transition networks, or RTNs for short. Things start getting really complicated once we start bouncing from one network to another, as in

16. The pen on the table in the living room with the blue cap.

but it is not yet important to keep track of how many times we have changed networks. Nevertheless, once the basics are grasped, the concept of *embedding* comes into play for the largest network, which maps out the patterns of sentence formation.

Figure 4: Prepositional phrase network.

The S Network

Figure 5 shows a limited network for generating or parsing sentences. It includes arcs that invoke other networks within them. Thus arc S1 represents within it the whole process of the NP network. Note that we could mark send arcs out of (c) and (d) – you can stop there or you can carry on along a new arc, as with intransitive verb sentences like 'Nicky laughed.', where all words are dealt with by state (c), or transitive ones with only one object like 'Wendy threw the ball', which run out of words at state (d). The network however puts these across a final 'jump' arc, either S7 or S8, into the end state (e). The final arc out of (e), the 'send' arc, is the only 'exit' from the network, and is needed for when we start adding extra rules, called *augmentations*.

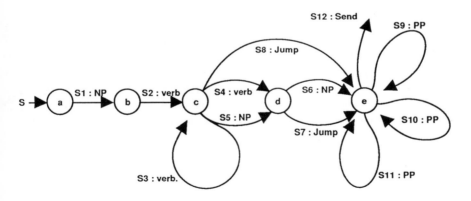

Figure 5: Sentence network.

The network is now complex enough to deal with verbal constructions involving passives, auxiliaries and all the tenses. The following are some of the sentences that can be dealt with:

17. My big brother must have been having a wild party at that time.
18. The card was given to me by a friend.
19. Helen will have been impressed with Chris.

With sentence 17, the sequence of arcs traversed is this: firstly, 'My big brother' traverses the 'NP' arc, S1, between (a) and (b); in the process travelling through the NP states (f), (g) (twice) and (h), using arcs NP1, NP3, NP4 and NP8 in the NP network. The next word, 'must' then traverses the arc S2 from (b) to (c), followed by 'have', 'been' and 'having', each of which traverses arc S3 round back to (c) again.

Next, the noun phrase 'a wild party' traverses sentence arc S5, (c) to (d), travelling through the NP network along the same route as 'My big brother' did. Remember, sentence arcs S1 and S5 each represent a traversal from the start of the NP network to its finish. We then 'jump' along S7 to (e). Finally, 'at that time' traverses sentence arc S9, S10 *or* S11. At present, it can pass along any of the three since each is marked as representing the PP network – they will be differentiated later. So this phrase travels round from (e) back to (e); through states (i) to (j) along PP1, which parses or generates 'at'; through the NP network (f), (g) and (h) along NP1 and NP4, leaving the NP network by NP7 to (k) – this deals with 'that time'; and then exiting the PP network by PP arc 3. After this prepositional phrase is finished with, the sentence exits the sentence network by arc S12.

You might notice that 'at that time' could have gone round the PP arc inside the NP network, NP7 from (h) round back to (h); but that would have meant a different sentence structure which had 'at that time' modifying the *party* rather than the *event* of its being held. There were also other possibilities for the route taken across the S network, but these would not have had a bearing on the tree structure of the sentence.

This is all well and good, but as yet we can still generate and recognise complete nonsense, so long as the words fit the pattern. Try fitting these across the network:

20. *Me leave having must try some book to the honour with her horse.
21. *Eagles goes Jeremy up our board.
22. *Robin sell done of this time in a order through Ed.

What we need are the following augmentations. Firstly, some restrictions on whether an arc can be traversed – called *conditions* ; secondly, somewhere to record all the information about the various elements of the sentence as we parse or generate it – labelled stores called *registers* ; these can be used to check for grammatical consistency (e.g. number agreement between different elements); and finally to do the 'writing' to these stores, we need instructions on each arc, called *actions*.

AUGMENTED TRANSITION NETWORKS (ATNs)

One of the earliest problems encountered with the phrase structure rules was the production of noun phrases where the determiner and noun did not match for number – one was singular, the other plural. It so happens that few if any adjectives in English cause complications of this kind, being invariable between singular and plural (cf. inflected languages like French) and between gender. The borrowed French word 'blond/blonde' might be cited as one exception. Many determiners can be used with singular or plural nouns, but some like 'a' or 'many' are specifically singular or plural. If, while traversing the NP network, we keep a record of the properties of the words matched so far, we can check the NP as we go along for internal consistency. The information can also be used in the S network to check that subject and verb agree for number. Thus we use *registers* to keep the 'features' (number and person), and 'roles' (determiner, head word(s) and describers). A register is a bit like a blackboard, or a string variable on a computer, in that you can write on it, read it later, add bits, or rub bits out. When you begin a particular traversal of the network the board is wiped clean and defaults are put in the feature registers.

To parse a sentence with an augmented network, you check that you satisfy the *conditions* of the relevant arcs, if any, and carry out the *actions*, if any, moving on to the next word in the sequence. Here are some conditions and actions for the NP network (Figure 3):

there are 'role' registers, showing the function of the word(s):
    [DETERMINER], [HEAD] and [DESCRIBERS]
and 'feature' registers:
    [NUMBER] (default=empty) and [PERSON] (default=3rd)

Here, an asterisk is used to represent 'all the words (including 'none') that have been parsed on this arc'.

arc   C = condition, A = Action
name

NP1   C: none (go straight across)
       A: set [DETERMINER] register to *
         set [NUMBER] register to number of * (singular or plural)
NP2   C: none (go straight across, don't tick off any words as 'matched')
       A: none (there is no [DETERMINER], so it remains empty, the default)
NP3   C: none
       A: append * to the [DESCRIBERS]
NP4   C: [NUMBER] is either empty or the same as that of this word
       A: set [HEAD] register to *
         set [NUMBER] register to the number of *
NP5   C: none
       A: set [HEAD] register to *
         set [NUMBER] and [PERSON] to the number and person of *
NP6   C: none
       A: set [HEAD] register to *
         set [NUMBER] to the number of *
NP7   C: none
       A: append the details of the PP registers(*), having traversed the PP
         network, to [DESCRIBERS]
NP8   C: none
       A: leave network successfully

Try running some noun phrases across the network. You will notice that nonsensical ones are still accepted as long as they are only ridiculous in meaning, not structure. So 'the giant blue pink miniature dead life' passes the test for grammaticality.

Augmented sentence network
If we 'augment' the sentence network with the additions below, we have a powerful parser that will deal with passives, direct and indirect objects, number and person agreement, and tenses (though the auxiliaries will still need unravelling).

Sentence network conditions and actions (see Figure 5: Sentence network.)

role (function) registers: [SUBJECT], [DIRECT_OBJECT], [INDIRECT_OBJECT], [MAIN_VERB], [AUXILIARIES], [MODIFIERS]; initially these are all empty.

feature registers: [VOICE] (default=active) and [MOOD] (default=declarative)

arc name	C = condition, A = action

S1　　C: none (go straight across)
　　　A: set [SUBJECT] register to *
S2　　C: either: * is a modal verb
　　　　　　or　:　* is a past-tense verb
　　　　　　or　:　* is an s-inflected verb and the [number] of [SUBJECT]
　　　　　　is singular and the [person] of [SUBJECT] is 3rd
　　　　　　or　:* is a non-s-inflected present-tense form
　　　　　　and either: the [number] of [SUBJECT] is Plural
　　　　　　　　　　or: the [person] of [SUBJECT] is 1st or 2nd
　　　A: Set [MAIN-VERB] register to *
S3　　C: [MAIN-VERB] is a form of 'be', 'do', 'have' or a modal auxiliary
　　　A: append the contents of the [MAIN-VERB] register to [AUXILI-ARIES] and replace them with *
S4　　C: * is a past participle and [MAIN-VERB] is a form of 'be'
　　　A: set [VOICE] to passive; append the contents of [MAIN-VERB] to [AUXILIARIES] and replace them with * ; set [DIRECT_OBJECT] to the contents of [SUBJECT] and replace [SUBJECT]'s contents with a dummy NP
S5　　C: none
　　　A: set [DIRECT_OBJECT] to *
S6　　C: none
　　　A: set [INDIRECT_OBJECT] to the contents of [DIRECT_OBJECT]; set [DIRECT_OBJECT] to *
S7　　C: none
　　　A: none (go straight through)
S8　　C: none
　　　A: none (go straight through)

S9   C: none
        A: append * to [MODIFIERS]
S10   C: [VOICE] is passive and [SUBJECT] is a dummy-NP and the
        preposition of * is 'by'
        A: set [SUBJECT] to the NP of *
S11   C: the preposition of * is 'to' or 'for' and [INDIRECT_OBJECT] is
        empty
        A: set [INDIRECT_OBJECT] to the NP of *
S12   C: if [INDIRECT_OBJECT] is not empty, then [MAIN-VERB] is
        ditransitive
        and if [INDIRECT_OBJECT] is empty but [DIRECT_OBJECT] is not,
        then [MAIN-VERB] is transitive
        and if [DIRECT_OBJECT] is empty, then [MAIN-VERB] is intransi-
        tive
        A: leave network successfully

Here are a couple of sentences that you can run across the network, with
their routes listed:

17. My big brother must have been having a wild party (jump) at that time. SEND
    [S1   ] [S2] [S3] [S3] [S3] [S4   ] [S7] [S9   ] [S12]
    [NP1][NP3][NP4]   [NP1][NP3] [NP4]   [PP1[PP2]
                                                                       [NP1][NP4]

18. The card was given (jump)   to me   by a   friend.
    [S1   ] [S2] [S4]   [S7]   [S11   ] [S10   ]
    [NP1][NP4]   [PP1][PP2] [PP1][PP2]
                                   [NP5]   [NP1] [NP4]

The S network will generate or match many sentences, and can be expanded upon
to include questions, subordinate clauses, co-ordinations, imperatives, negatives
and, given enough space, any possible combination of words. Idiomatic
constructions could be built in too, but it would be more economical to check for
them separately by trying to match idiom patterns to the sentence in a separate
algorithm. The network as it stands will deal with quite complex clauses, but has
limitations and will still accept 'wrong' constructions. One of the simplest is the
unlimited acceptance of auxiliary verbs, and a count limit of '5 passes of arc 3'
would at least cut down the potential number of wrong sentences, while still
accepting right ones like

23. She will have been trying keeping going.

Some grammars would reject this sentence as ungrammatical, and would impose a lower count limit.

Alternative approaches

As you can see, at present the same sentence can go through the network successfully by several different routes, coming up with differing analyses. Sometimes the sentence may be genuinely ambiguous, even to a human eye, but in others, we can use probability to suggest the analysis most likely to be right. This is done by comparing the different outputs with other previous analyses and seeing which constructions occur most often. We could use information gleaned from corpus research (see chapter 2) on 'collocation', that is, which words tend to occur together, to suggest the most likely interpretation. As an example, with a sentence like

24. The guard posts shot by the truck.

we could end up with:

(a) [SUBJECT]:the guard posts [MAIN-VERB]: shot [MODIFIERS]: by the truck
    (...'And the truck then crashed through the gates of the compound')

or:

(b) [SUBJECT]:the guard [MAIN-VERB]:posts [DIRECT-OBJECT]:shot [MODIFIERS]: by the truck
    (...'He always stores spare ammunition near his transport.')

Here, the most probable interpretation is the first (given no other context). The computer might use information like the fact that 'shot' and 'by' collocate more often than 'post' and 'shot', to conclude that the first is the better guess. With shortened, elided sentences, the computer will need to be programmed with an ability to use some form of deductive reasoning, to use what information it has already gained from previous input. It might be able to reconstruct the full form of a shortened sentence by looking for similar key words in preceding sentences or use the presence of patterns or words to guess at the full 'underlying' sentence, as in a question and answer;-

25. (a) 'What was John doing yesterday down by the lake at 4pm in a wetsuit?'

    (b) 'He was going waterskiing' (yesterday down by the lake at 4pm in a wetsuit).

By comparing the features in the sentences (the tense, both subjects being male and singular, the form of question followed by answer) we can make a guess at the missing information in (b). Actually 'understanding' natural language is something we can only touch on. There are philosophical questions as to what exactly constitutes comprehension. We can work out the structure of a sentence without understanding it:

26. The glibble drexpots have scrampled in the froon.

(i.e. we could answer the question 'Who did what, and where?'), and likewise guess at the intended meaning of other sequences:

27. Percy driving car tonight far will.

where each word carries an implication of sorts. Some research has focused on attempting to break down words into all the separate nuances of meaning they carry, in order to treat them as merely containing a number of manipulable units of basic meaning. We can certainly break down words like 'anti-disestablish-ment--ari-an-ism', but we can also try the more difficult task of disassembling words to separate every single feature of meaning. We could say there is a scale of formality between 'shake off this mortal coil', 'die', and 'kick the bucket', marking on a scale of one to ten, and class all similar constructions under a group titled 'DIE'. We could also draw up a scale from 'dead' to 'ill', to 'well' to 'vibrant', headed 'HEALTH', moving one step further towards breaking down language into its meaning. But the question is, if we do achieve a machine that passes Turing's test for pretending to think like a human, will it truly understand what it is saying?

SUGGESTIONS FOR FURTHER READING

The following go into more detail about various subjects discussed in this chapter.

1. E.K. Brown and J.E. Miller, *Syntax: A Linguistic Introduction to Sentence Structure* (Hutchinson University Library, 1980). A good introduction to tree structures, generative phrase structure grammars and the hierarchical structure of language.

2. Terry Winograd, *Language as a Cognitive Process (Vol.1: Syntax)* (Addison-Wesley, 1983). A very comprehensive explanation of many of the principles involved in this chapter, including recognition procedures, phrase structure grammars and transition networks. The best in its field.

3. John Haugeland (ed.), *Mind Design – Philosophy, Psychology, Artificial Intelligence* (MIT Press, 1981). A good series of articles on the philosophy behind NLP and AI.

4. Philip Barker, *Basic Principles of Human-Computer Interface Design* (Hutchinson Computer Studies Series, 1989).

5 Speech Production Modelling and Speech Synthesis

CELIA SCULLY and SANDRA WHITESIDE

The intriguing idea of a machine that can speak has challenged researchers for many years, probably for many centuries. A synthetic voice might inspire awe if made to issue from a statue, which is what the earliest scientists in this field aimed for; it could be of practical day-to-day value for communicating information from a computer by telephone and for human–machine communication in general; it could improve the quality of life for someone whose own speech-producing capabilities were disabled in some way; it could make toys and games more realistic. Artificial voices that give warnings or advice, in cars for example, are already familiar; a controlled range of voice types might be useful as a reference for use in medical diagnosis. Finally, in work in our own field, we are interested in synthesis because of the light it may shed on natural speech: a greater understanding of this, the most frequently used mode of communication between people, is a worthwhile aim in its own right, and in addition synthetic speech can be valuable in helping us to find out by means of perception experiments how the human brain recognises speech. The use of computers to control speech synthesis is one of the longest established applications of computers in our field.

Birds can fly, but machines produced by humans to do the same thing do not look at all like birds. Planes stay up in the air because they can exploit in some way the basic physical principles of flight; it is the underlying maths that a model must copy. The same sort of idea applies in the case of synthetic speech: the machines that we discuss here do not look at all like humans, but they do copy in one way or another the physical processes involved in human speech production. In this chapter, after a short explanation of how speech is produced, we explain firstly how we use computers to model that production process, then go on to describe the more widely known approach to speech synthesis that simply aims to copy the resulting sounds.

THE PRODUCTION OF SPEECH

Speech is such an everyday activity and it is, apparently, so easily acquired by the vast majority of children that most of us are likely to think of it as simple and easy to copy. But this is far from true: just to produce an 'ah' sound demands skilful co-ordination of several actions and an experience-based knowledge of several different kinds of physical process. Let us consider what these processes are – the different stages that are gone through in speaking. They can be thought of as a logically connected sequence, even though in real life only a fraction of a second elapses between the idea – the linguistic message – in a speaker's brain and the emergence of a sound wave which carries the message to listeners.

First, inside the speaker's central nervous system, the idea is assembled into a particular sequence of words. Inside the central nervous system, instructions are sent to many different muscles – breathing muscles, larynx muscles and facial muscles – with the correct timing patterns to ensure that the sounds will emerge in the right order for that word sequence. The muscles provide the most important forces to move some solid structures: the lungs and chest walls, the larynx, the tongue, the jaw, the lips and the soft palate which separates the nose from the upper throat. Actually, we need to make slightly finer distinctions and so draw up a list of about ten to fifteen articulators, solid structures each of which can be moved somewhat independently of the others. All the sounds used in speech come from air movement, mainly air being breathed out of the lungs. Unlike ordinary breathing, for speech the air comes out of the lungs in a slow controlled flow and there is always at least one severe obstruction to that flow, somewhere between the lungs and the nose and mouth outlets.

At these obstructions a smoothly flowing, silent stream of air speeds up and the flow becomes turbulent, with eddies, like a river flowing between wide banks and then flowing at high speed through a narrow gorge. Just as water will flow from a higher to a lower level, air will flow from a region where the air pressure is higher, with the air molecules packed more closely together, to a region of lower air pressure. During speech, the air just below the larynx and throughout the trachea, bronchial tubes and lungs is raised above the pressure of the atmosphere around the speaker. This difference of pressure drives the air through the larynx. The vocal folds, like a tiny pair of lips running from front to back in the larynx, will vibrate if they are brought together and tensed in the right way. A similar effect can be produced with the lips or by blowing through two sheets of paper held close together. The vocal folds are smaller than the lips and they vibrate at a higher rate. This vibration is called *voicing* or *voice* ; it is heard as having a pitch and provides the tune or intonation for speech; it has the carrying power which other kinds of sounds made in speech do not have. But the two other ways of turning a silent airstream into sound are important also: the eddies formed as a jet of air issues at high speed from a narrow obstructed portion is called *turbulence noise*; it is a hissing irregular sound without a clear note, rather like steam issuing from a kettle or valve. The sudden air movement to equalise air pressure when two regions of different pressure are suddenly linked is called a *transient*; this is a sudden short-lasting burst of sound, rather like a bottle being uncorked. Voice, turbulence noise and transient are the sound sources of speech.

From these three types of sound, with silence as a fourth type, thousands of different speech sounds are produced. The phenomenon which modifies the sound sources to create this variety is *resonance* : this is the property which all objects possess of sounding out at characteristic notes if struck. Plasticine and lead are not good resonators, but many other materials are; the phenomenon of resonance forms the basis for most musical instruments, whether in strings, blocks, bells or air-filled pipes. The resonators of speech production are in this last category: the air trapped inside the speaker's throat, nose and mouth, called the *vocal tract*, sings out at its characteristic notes when it is given a kind of negative tap. This tap is the sudden cutting off of the air as the vocal folds close sharply once in each of their vibration cycles. Vowel sounds can be distinguished because they have different shaped resonators; the voice source of sound is the same for all of them, but it is modified differently for each vowel sound, so that each vowel sound has its own characteristic combination of prominent notes, or *formants*. For example [i:] as in 'see' has a low note for its first formant (F1) then a gap, with several formants – F2, F3 and F4 – close together at high notes. [ɑ:] 'ah' has two formants – F1 and F2 – close together in the middle of the range of notes. Turbulence noise also is modified by resonance to make the various voiceless fricative sounds: [s], [f], [ʃ] as in 'show' and [θ] as in 'thin'. Speech sounds can have more than one sound source: [z] for example has voicing and also turbulence noise. In general, vowels have a relatively unconstricted air passage above the larynx while consonants have a severe narrowing or complete closure somewhere in the vocal tract.

Sound sources and their modification by resonance constitute the acoustic processes of speech production. As a result, an air disturbance with very small, rapid changes of air pressure called a soundwave is radiated away from the speaker. This speech soundwave emerges mainly from the speaker's mouth and nostrils, but also from the throat walls and other face and chest surfaces. This is the final output of the long chain of events needed to produce speech; it is the output speech signal.

COPYING THE SPEECH PRODUCTION PROCESS

Line analog synthesis

As we said at the beginning, there are two distinct ways of copying the final links in the chain of processes outlined above, to give synthetic speech; in *terminal analog* synthesis the main object is to simulate the sounds of human speech, while *line analog* synthesis copies the source-resonator processes as they happen inside the vocal tract. In a line analog synthesiser, sources are controlled separately, but the resonators or formants are not. From an audio recording of speech a possible vocal tract tube shape is obtained, with a particular combination of resonances or formants. At each time moment a combination of formants is thus defined in the synthesiser. In this way the formants are constrained to conform to combinations and changes of total pattern with time that are actually possible in real speech.

It is logical to go even further back in the chain of processes to find a starting point for the synthesiser's copy or model of real speech. It seems reasonable to suppose that the nearer the synthesiser machine comes to representing all of the natural processes and the chain of events, the more closely it will resemble real speech – automatically, not by a great number of complicated rules or detailed descriptions.

The crucial point is that speech is not just a sequence of sounds: it is sounds produced in a specific way from a particular kind of (human) machine or system. So speech sounds have special properties. For example, the changing pattern of resonances or formants of real speech reflects movements of the solid articulators such as the main body of the tongue which moves slowly, or the tip of the tongue which moves more rapidly. The speed of formant patterns changing with time reflect these underlying movement constraints.

Another aspect of the special nature of speech sounds is that they are rich and complicated as sound patterns. One of the reasons for this is the nature of the movements of the articulators. There are around forty basic units *(phonemes)* of a language such as English, but there are not forty fixed, unvarying blocks of sound to go with these linguistic units. The total set of articulators does not jump or move simultaneously from one phoneme state to the next phoneme state; instead, the different articulators move at different times, skilfully co-ordinated with each other to ensure that no extra sounds creep in and that no essential sounds are left out. The links between successive phoneme units are of the essence in speech production, more so than the segments characteristic of each phoneme unit on its own. So the actions and the resultant sound patterns for a single phoneme vary greatly depending on its context – the phonemes next to it.

Another cause of richness and complexity is the fact that all speech sounds are made by a moving airstream, as described above. This airstream flows through the whole of the respiratory tract from the lungs, up through the larynx and through the vocal tract. Thus all the various sound sources, even though they arise at different points along the respiratory tract, are connected by the airstream and by the aerodynamic processes. In addition, the changing resonator shape, the air-filled tube, affects the airstream and so the sound sources. A simple change of position of one articulator can mean that several features of the speech sound change together. The bewildering complexity of the speech sounds is not random; it is rule-governed and arises, in part at least, from the physical processes used in making the sounds. The complex variations with context observed for speech and the variability of the patterns when a word is repeated seem to be useful for human listeners, yet they present severe problems to speech recognition devices. So a better understanding of the physical processes and how they influence the combinations of sound patterns found in speech might be useful for automatic speech recognition too.

What is generally referred to as *articulatory speech synthesis* is the representation of the physical processes, from articulation onwards, in a computer model from which synthetic speech is output. How do computers play a part in all of this? The answer is that they are essential for calculating conditions and effects over and over again, first at one time point, then at the next time point, then at the next, all the way through the time span to be modelled.

We began this chapter by trying to demonstrate that speech production is not at all simple; now we are considering a very simplified computational representation of the real speech processes. As in the example of bird or aeroplane flight, the maths must be correct, even if, as in our modelling, it is the maths in a simplified form: equations are needed to represent the flow of air from the lungs, through the larynx and into and out of the vocal tract. Basic physical laws, notably that air cannot disappear, must be incorporated: air flowing into the vocal tract from the larynx partly flows through the mouth and nose and is partly used up if the vocal tract enclosed volume space enlarges and if the air pressure inside this enclosed vocal tract volume rises, as during [s], [v], [p] or [g], for example. This aerodynamic system is unified: a set of equations has to be solved simultaneously. Very small time steps must be taken, otherwise the calculations swing wildly from too small to too big. Fortunately, methods of solving equations have been developed and are available from a package called the NAG (Numerical Algorithms Group) library. We can produce graphs with the model to show how the airflow in and out of the mouth changes with time and how the air pressure in the vocal tract rises and falls. These can be compared with the corresponding traces obtained from a real speaker. If they do not match well, we go back to the articulatory stage of the model and modify the movement patterns for the articulators, then try the aerodynamics again.

A great advantage of representing the aerodynamic processes in a model is that one can calculate the air pressure in the trachea, under the larynx: this is very important in speech but very difficult to find out about in real speech even with a doctor to help. Perhaps the most severe limitation on current efforts to produce synthetic speech by articulatory synthesis is the very great difficulty of obtaining sufficient information about the articulators and their movement paths in real speech. Some exciting new techniques are being developed, involving ultrasound, magnetic emitters and detectors, optical movement detectors and so on, but a modeller must nevertheless base his or her articulatory simulation on tiny scraps of data and hints as to how the actions of real speech might be organised. In our modelling, articulation is not described through fundamental physical principles *(dynamics)*, but through descriptions which are meant to match paths observed in natural speech *(kinematics)*.

A computer is essential for the rather tricky aerodynamic calculations. It is essential also for the many simple but repetitive calculations needed to describe changes in shape of the lungs, the larynx and the different portions of the vocal tract. The calculations need to be performed every 10 or preferably every 5 thousandths of a second (ms); we chose the smaller 5 ms sample time. It is helpful to state a generalised shape for an articulatory gesture or transition and then leave the computer to fill in the detailed values through much arithmetic. But what would be a sensible approximation to the paths of natural speech? For an answer we have had to look at the available data, almost entirely cineradiographic (X-ray films) published in the 1960s. It is easy to talk about the way articulators move, but quantitative computer modelling has the disciplining effect of forcing the investigator to state this precisely, not vaguely. It appeared that a bigger distance moved did not necessarily take a longer time. We decided to simplify by saying that the same time would be taken by a given articulator to move a small or a big distance. This articulatory transition consisted of the following phases: starting from rest, accelerating to maximum velocity, decelerating down to rest again. Recently published research papers have supported our original choice, though a better approximation to real speech now seems to be maximum velocity increasing in proportion to the distance and giving a slightly longer total time for a transition of bigger distance. So articulatory models should change as more is learned about natural speech.

When we attempt to copy a person's production of a particular word of English, we match the actions in the model to those of natural speech, in so far as we can. We go through the various processes by means of computer programs which have files as their outputs, to be fed into the next stage of the model.

Finally, we obtain a sequence of numbers which represents a radiated soundwave as if it had been recorded by a microphone near the synthetic speaker. Only at this point do we leave the numerical, sampled approach of the computer. The digitally sampled soundwave is fed through a *D to A (digital to analog) converter*, low-pass filtered to avoid the distortion called *aliasing*, then recorded on an audio tape recorder. Our early attempts are inevitably extremely bad. Much trial and error with auditory monitoring is needed to improve the match between the synthetic and the real target speech. In going through these long, slow simulations of a sequence of processes which happen together and almost instantaneously in natural speech, we learn a lot about the tasks confronting real speakers during speech acquisition. Adults have developed their speech production skills so well over so many years that they are not aware of the very great problems they have overcome. Also, they are set in their ways and cannot produce intermediate actions; with our model we can make the 'speaker' use a series of different co-ordinations, between the larynx and the tongue for example, and then ask why particular co-ordinations are used in real speech.

One aspect has hit us forcibly: in our computer system we have a long delay between the actions and the resulting sounds – an extreme case of delayed auditory feedback. We do hear the results eventually, but it is difficult for us to make enough attempts at a particular auditory goal to get really close to it. We learn to sympathise deeply with profoundly deaf children who also suffer deprivations of auditory feedback. We should not ask why they get this or that wrong in speech; rather we should ask how it is that they get anything right. We should like to develop this composite model of speech production processes further and use it to look at several kinds of disordered speech production. At present we are using it to study the production of fricatives, and we are trying to make the model simulate specific speakers, by obtaining as much information as possible about their production of these speech sounds, in a European collaborative project.

TERMINAL ANALOG SYNTHESIS

Copying the speech wave

We have described the type of synthesis (line analog and articulatory synthesis) which sets out to model the human speech production process. Many researchers, however, feel that the highest priority should be given to producing the best possible (most human-sounding) synthetic speech by whatever is the most efficient means available. This approach is particularly relevant for practical applications in two areas. Firstly, in commercial and industrial applications the cost-effectiveness and simplicity of the technology is very important, and some terminal analog synthesisers can be made very cheaply and compactly. Secondly, for experimental work in speech perception we want to be able to produce synthetic speech in a way that allows us to make fine adjustments to many different aspects of the speech, and terminal analog synthesisers are usually preferred for this because they tend to be simpler and easier to use than line analog synthesisers.

If you want to understand how terminal analog synthesis works it is necessary to go into some detail about the different designs that are in use, and to examine different ways of controlling the synthesis process. We will concentrate on *formant synthesis*, since this is the most widely used. We explained earlier that formants are the characteristic areas of energy produced by resonances in the vocal tract, and one of the synthesiser's main jobs is to produce these formants under the control of the user and the computer. There are two basic designs of formant synthesiser (we say there are two 'architectures'): one is called a *parallel* synthesiser and the other a *series* or *cascade* synthesiser. In both cases, we have to be able to control the *source* of the sound being synthesised and the settings for the formants: as we explained earlier, speech sounds have to have a source, such as *voicing* (as for vowels) or turbulence noise (as for voiceless fricatives such as the [s], [ʃ] of 'see', 'she'); in addition, all sounds have a small number of important formants, and these vary in frequency and amplitude (they also vary in *bandwidth*, but we will not worry about that here). Figures 1 and 2 show how the different architectures are organised: in both cases the synthesis process begins with the generation of the source excitation, but while in the parallel design, the filters that control the formant frequencies and amplitudes are all linked simultaneously (i.e. are in parallel), the series architecture involves passing the signal from one stage to the next. It is generally claimed that this is closer to the human speech production process, at least for vowels. However, as we explained above, that is not the main object in terminal analog synthesis.

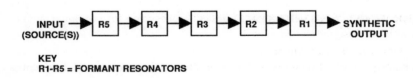

KEY
R1-R5 = FORMANT RESONATORS

Figure 1: A schematic representation of a cascade-connected formant synthesiser.

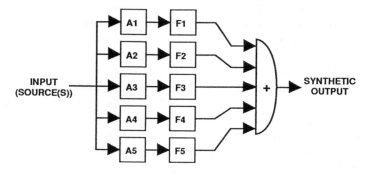

KEY
A1-A5 = Amplitude controls for formant resonators
F1-F5 = Formant resonators

Figure 2: A schematic representation of a parallel-connected formant synthesiser.

Controlling formant synthesisers

Terminal analog synthesisers existed well before laboratory computers, and a number of ingenious techniques were devised for controlling them in order to create the desired output signal. These included playing an organ-type keyboard, painting curves and lines on glass slides or sheets of plastic, and setting knobs and switches on large manual control panels. Nowadays computers do all the detailed control work for us, and the human scientist simply has to devise the most convenient way to plan the work. One thing that all synthesis systems share is that before you can make a start on producing synthetic speech, detailed analysis of real human speech is necessary: the alternative would be to work towards a desired utterance by trial and error, and apart from the fact that this would be very time consuming you would have to be able to listen objectively to dozens or perhaps hundreds of different versions of the synthetic speech. This is virtually impossible to do. In some cases it is possible to make use of the analysis done by someone else, as we will explain. The techniques used for computer analysis of speech are described in chapter 3.

One approach to synthesis that is widely found in speech laboratories is *copy synthesis*, where the investigator is interested in working in fine detail on simulating human speech and specifying the precise parameter values necessary to produce the desired result. In our laboratory, for example, we are working on the problem of synthesising a realistic-sounding female voice, something that requires a great deal of painstaking work. Copy synthesis is sometimes known as *synthesis by analysis* or *analysis-resynthesis*. It is possible to do copy synthesis with the preliminary analysis being done completely automatically by the computer (*automatic copy synthesis with passive user participation*). The results of the acoustic analysis are stored in a file of parameter values that are subsequently used to control the synthesiser. This may sound rather pointless, and if the computer always got a perfect result it probably would be; however, speech is full of surprises and we can learn a lot by studying where automatic processes break down. When the process works satisfactorily, we gain further knowledge about how to do formant synthesis. More commonly found, though, is *synthesis-by-analysis with active user participation*. In this method, also, the computer is used to analyse a speech signal. However, this time the user manually extracts relevant parameter values and writes them to a parameter file which is stored by the computer. This process is more time consuming and it is up to the user to decide how often to update the parameter information. A more regular update ensures smoother changes in frequency and amplitude and reduces the risk of clicks or 'glitches' that might occur with sudden changes. The parameter values are then read from the stored file and used by the synthesiser to produce synthetic speech. The synthetic speech is digitised and stored in the computer as a file of numbers. As before, these need to undergo digital-to-analog conversion before the user can listen to whether his or her interpretation of the analysis has been successful.

The whole interaction may involve the use of computer graphics, and this helps keep the user informed of the parameters controlling the synthesiser. There may also be additional facilities for the user to play back sections of the synthetic speech token as desired. This is an exciting exercise because it is then possible to locate accurately where the synthesis might have gone wrong. It makes the computer almost indispensable.

Text-to-speech synthesis and synthesis-by-rule

For many commercial and industrial applications of synthetic speech the major research goal is to develop systems that make the generation of speech sounds as rapid and automatic as possible. Text-to-speech systems are the ultimate stage of this development: in these, users are simply able to type in ordinary text and this is transformed automatically into a string of synthetic speech. The computer controls the entire process.

The two main steps involved are: (1) linguistic processing, where text is converted into phonemes (sounds) and intonation patterns, and (2) synthesis of the appropriate speech waveform. For many languages, converting from the letters of written text to the phonemes of speech presents few problems, but for English the problems are extremely serious. Of course, few humans manage a complete command of the spelling system of English. The conversion problems go much deeper than the obvious cases like words that end in '-ough': for example, English spelling does not show how some words have 'weak' and 'strong' pronunciation forms, so that 'there' is likely to be pronounced like 'the' in the sentence 'There could be', but like 'their' in 'There you are'. The commonest vowel in English speech, the 'schwa' vowel that is pronounced at the beginning of 'about' and at the end of 'opera' has no particular spelling equivalent; in addition, the text-to-speech conversion program must be able to cope with the movements of stress and the changes in vowel quality that go with it (for example, consider the differences in the syllables making up the following group of words: 'photograph', 'photography', 'photographic'). When the text has been converted into phoneme symbols, the synthesis process requires an elaborate set of rules that tell the synthesiser how the phonemes are to be joined together, since the context in which a sound occurs has a profound effect on the sound itself, and the *transitions* between phonemes must be carefully controlled. This part of the process is known as *synthesis-by-rule*, and at present such synthesis sounds unmistakably machine-like, unlike copy synthesis which at its best can sound as human as a tape-recording. You can hear synthesis-by-rule speech in some of the telephone bank enquiry systems that have been installed recently. One of the most satisfying applications of the technology is that of reading machines for the blind, where the machine recognises the letters in the text of the book or paper, carries out text-to-phoneme conversion and then uses synthesis-by-rule to 'speak' what it has 'read'.

Synthesis-by-rule does not necessarily proceed phoneme-by-phoneme: some researchers have achieved good results with *diphone synthesis* or *demisyllable* synthesis (these units were referred to in chapter 3). Diphones are obtained by dividing a speech waveform into pairs of phoneme-sized units so that the transitions between each phoneme are preserved. Demisyllables are obtained by dividing the syllable into half during the steadiest portion of the vowel. The storage of demisyllables and diphones is in the form of numbers that will be used to control the synthesiser. The stored demisyllables and diphones are pulled out of storage and joined together ('concatenated') when required. This of course requires a lot of the computer's available memory for storage. So, for example, if the word 'stool' were to be synthesised the diphones [=s] - [st] - [tu] - [ul - [l=] (where the symbol '=' denotes silence) would be used; in the case of demisyllables, [= stu] - [ul =] would be used.

There are, then, many ways of generating synthetic speech and many ways of controlling the process with a computer. In spite of the great amount of research that has been carried out over recent decades, there is still a great deal more to be done before we can feel that we really understand how to simulate human speech and the way in which it is produced.

SUGGESTIONS FOR FURTHER READING

There are sections on human speech production, the process which articulatory synthesis tries to mimic, in many introductory textbooks, for example G.J. Borden and K.S. Harris, *A Speech Science Primer* (Baltimore: Williams and Wilkins, 2nd edn, 1984).

R. Linggard, *Electronic Speech Synthesis* (Cambridge University Press, 1985) deals with many different approaches to synthetic speech, including both acoustic and articulatory synthesis. There is some difficult maths in places, but this is a good introduction to the whole field of synthesis. J. Allen, M.S. Hunnicutt and D. Klatt, *From Text to Speech: The MITalk System* (Cambridge University Press, 1987) describes one kind of synthesis in detail. There is a clear and concise account of speech production and its representation in models, as well as chapters on synthesis from stored human speech components and speech synthesis-by-rule.

6   Machine Translation

GEOFFREY SAMPSON

Translating was one of the first tasks that people ever thought of applying computers to – which seems paradoxical, because it is perhaps the most difficult of all current computer applications. The first successful operation of a stored-program electronic computer took place at the University of Manchester in June 1948. Within weeks Alan Turing, the mathematician who had as good a claim as anyone to be regarded as the computer's inventor, was drawing up a list of potential uses for his brainchild: 'Translation of languages' was item three. The invention of the computer had sprung out of work during the Second World War on machines for cracking German and Japanese ciphers; to many of the people involved, translating seemed a natural extension of that work. The analogy was very explicit in a memorandum circulated in 1949 by the American Warren Weaver, which launched machine translation as a widespread research goal:

> it is very tempting to say that a book written in Chinese is simply a book written in English which was coded into the 'Chinese code'. If we have useful methods for solving almost any cryptographic problem, may it not be that ... we already have useful methods for translation?

We would not nowadays see analogies between translating and decoding as very convincing. Ideas about language have changed, and these changing ideas have been reflected in the development of machine translation, or MT as it is commonly called. Quite a good way to get a grasp of the problems involved in translating by computer is to begin with a brief look at the history of the subject; it has not been a smooth one.

After Warren Weaver's memorandum, work on the development of MT systems got under way in many places, particularly in the USA but also in Britain and elsewhere; and in the years around 1960 MT became a hot topic, lavishly funded by governments and a glamorous research area in the eyes of the general public. According to the prevailing assumption, it would only be a few years before computers were translating at essentially the same level as humans – perhaps missing some literary nuances, but certainly producing outputs that were quite satisfactory for scientific or commercial purposes. Everyone in those days knew the jokes about MT that went the rounds, like the computer which translated 'The spirit is willing but the flesh is weak' into Russian as 'The vodka is good but the meat has gone off'.

One dramatic event fuelled the urgency with which MT research was pressed forward in those years: the Soviet Union's launch in 1957 of Sputnik, the first artificial satellite, and the heartsearching this triggered among Americans. Here was a nation which, until that date, most Americans had dismissed as technologically primitive and hampered by an obnoxious political system, but which suddenly demonstrated that it could beat the Americans at their own high-tech game. What else had the Russians got up their sleeve? The US taxpayer wanted answers, and was very willing to pay for MT if that could speed the goal of adequately monitoring the Soviet threat. And so MT in those early years was oriented predominantly towards scientific and military documents, and towards one pair of languages: Russian to English.

To give an idea of the standards achieved, I show below a sample of output from the US Air Force Automatic Translator Mark 2, which came on line in 1964. The extracts shown are translated from a Russian paper on medical aspects of space travel. Where the system cannot choose between alternative translations, it prints both, separated by an oblique (the Russian word *mir* means both 'world' and 'peace'). Readers familiar with Russian will spot characteristic features of its syntax that the computer has failed to anglicise. For instance, Russian has no articles, and the translation system is almost never able to work out where 'the' or 'a' needs to be supplied in the English text.

> Biological experiments, conducted on different space aircraft/ vehicles, astrophysical space research and flights of Soviet and American astronauts with/from sufficient convincingness showed that short-term orbital flights lower than radiation belts of earth in the absence of heightened solar activity in radiation ratio are safe. Obtained by astronauts of dose of radiation at the expense of primary cosmic radiation and radiation of external radiation belt are so small that cannot render harmful influence on organism of person.

... Thus, consideration of certain from basic radiobiological problems shows that in given region still very many unsolved questions. This and intelligibly, since space radiobiology is very young division of young science – space biology. However is base to trust that jointly scientists of different specialities of various countries of world/peace radiobiological investigations in outer space will be successfully continued and expanded.

Clearly, the technology had some way to go; but research was advancing fast. And then quite suddenly, in 1966, it stopped. For many years after that date MT was a dead duck. What killed it was an enquiry commissioned by the US Academy of Sciences and published as the ALPAC Report, after the initials of the committee which carried out the enquiry – the Automatic Language Processing Advisory Committee. The committee complained, first, that after several years' work the results of contemporary MT systems were not really very good, and they saw reasons to believe that they might never get much better (a point to which we shall return). Furthermore, the economics of MT was unfavourable. Translating by machine, badly, was expensive. In the 1960s, computers were massive, extremely costly devices – a university might own just one; and computer time was correspondingly dear. Human translators, on the other hand, were numerous and cheap: the committee found that Washington, D.C. contained many people qualified to translate Russian and eager to do such work for modest rates of pay – less per thousand words than computer translation was costing. But the most damning point of all related to the demand rather than the supply side of the translating equation: the people who used translated material were already at full stretch. '... all the Soviet literature for which there is any obvious demand is being translated ... if more material were translated, analysts would not be available to utilize it'. As a commercially viable proposition, MT apparently had little to be said for it, and research on the subject ceased almost everywhere.

In the late 1970s it revived; by now MT is as flourishing an activity as it has ever been. What has changed?

Many factors have altered, most obviously the economics of the process. Over the decades, as the cost of human labour and most other things has risen, the cost of computing has plummeted: the home micro that a youngster buys in a department store today is the equivalent of machines that research scientists queued to use in 1960. If computers can translate, it is inconceivable now that they could be undercut on cost by humans. And the typical customers for automatic translation have changed. The economic success of Western Europe has increased demand for translation in commerce and industry, while novel political arrangements have made multilingualism a newly significant phenomenon. Canada was always officially a bilingual country, but only since the 1960s have Canadian governments given French an important role alongside English in Canadian public life. As the European Community becomes increasingly integrated, it is turning into an unprecedented phenomenon: a state with nine official languages, no one of which takes legal precedence.

It was a Canadian development which changed people's minds about the value of MT in the late 1970s, when for the first time the use of computers in a practical translation situation changed from an aspiration into a routine reality. MT research in Canada never closed down after 1966 as it did in the USA. In the 1970s a group at the University of Montreal created the TAUM-METEO system for translating weather forecasts from English to French, and since 1977 TAUM-METEO has been the normal means by which French versions of Canadian public weather forecasts are produced on a daily basis. (*Météo* is French for weather forecast, and TAUM stands for Traduction Automatique de l'Université de Montréal.) Weather forecasts are a natural for MT: the vocabulary is extremely limited and predictable, and even the grammar is quite restricted (when did you see a question in a weather forecast?). Success with weather forecasts is a long way short of total success; but the achievements of TAUM--METEO changed the nature of the debate about MT. People no longer asked, as they had earlier, 'Is automatic translation possible?', since some automatic translation was already happening. Instead they started asking 'What kinds of text can reasonably be handed over to machine translation? How good is MT, and how costly are the practical consequences of a given level of errors, in a given class of documents?' Automatic translation will never be perfect, but then humans do not translate perfectly either – though, to date, humans are certainly far better at the job.

While a Canadian development showed that MT is possible, European circumstances in particular destroyed the argument that MT is pointless because of shortage of manpower to make use of extra translated material. Within the EC, vast quantities of low-level documentation – committee minutes or the like – must by law be translated into the nine EC languages, irrespective of whether the translations will be read. In many cases they quite likely will not be read: if (say) the Danish delegate needs to check an item then in practice he will read the English or French original without waiting for the Danish version to emerge from the translating pool, but by law that Danish version must still be produced. This work is both expensive and extremely tedious and unchallenging for the human translator; automating the translation of at least the less sensitive grades of documentation seems a boon to all concerned. It is little wonder that the EC has been one of the chief patrons of MT research. From 1976 onwards it invested in the Systran system, developed by the Czech Peter Toma; by 1981 English–French, French–English, and English–Italian versions of Systran came into routine use within the European Commission, and work began on further language pairs. But in the longer term the EC sees Systran as a stop gap, pending development of its own Eurotra system, which is intended to offer translation between *any* pair of EC languages. Initiated in 1979, Eurotra became one of the largest single information technology research efforts in the world, employing more than a hundred full-time researchers at various locations throughout the Community.

With hindsight we can see that the ALPAC Committee set its sights too high. The prose in the sample translation from a Russian space medicine paper was certainly pretty awful: but, if you are an English-speaking scientist wanting to scan quickly through hundreds of Soviet articles in order to pick out the two or three that are worth submitting to the expensive process of human translation, then the computer translation may be quite good enough for the purpose. In the 1980s, the German company Siemens invested heavily in MT, and at one point they carried out a cost/benefit study. Their ordinary, all-human translating organisation used two grades of translator: low-paid juniors, who produced first drafts, and higher-paid seniors who revised and polished the juniors' output into an acceptable final form. Siemens compared this with an alternative arrangement in which the junior but not the senior translators were replaced by Siemens' German-to-English MT system METAL. The automatic system produced drafts that were much worse than those of the junior translators; but the productivity of the experimental arrangement as a whole was nevertheless higher than that of the traditional arrangement, for an unforeseen reason. Senior translators correcting the work of human colleagues feel inhibited about making too many changes: they spend expensive minutes seeking the minimal alterations to the junior's draft that they can allow to pass. Faced with a machine-generated draft, on the other hand, psychological constraints disappear, and they make radical changes to the text rapidly and efficiently. Thus, paradoxically, poor machine translation actually proved to be more valuable to Siemens than better quality human translation.

Indeed, it is clear that computers can greatly improve productivity in a translating organisation without necessarily doing anything that could be called translation at all. The ALPAC Report noted that professional translators in practice spend between one-quarter and three-quarters of their working time (depending on the nature of the material) on vocabulary problems – essentially, looking up words in dictionaries and other works of reference. Producing a printed dictionary covering the vocabulary of a specialised technical field is a very expensive process, and one with such a long lead time that the books tend to be out of date from the day of publication. Furthermore, flicking through the pages of a shelf-ful of reference works is a time consuming activity. It is much cheaper and easier to give translators access through a computer terminal to terminology banks which can be updated in seconds rather than years. Nowadays, the window and mouse facilities of modern computer workstations are harnessed to make all aspects of the human translator's task more efficient than they were when everything had to be done using ink and paper. Not just dictionary lookup but preparation and editing of the translated text can be done on screen, using features such as parallel source and target texts in adjacent windows to make comparison simple. Computer applications of these kinds are called machine--aided translation (MAT).

Returning to machine translation proper: at the same time as economic factors were changing the prospects of MT, new intellectual developments were suggesting that people had been too pessimistic in assessing what MT could ultimately hope to achieve. We saw that the ALPAC Report complained in 1966 not just that contemporary MT was poor (which was true enough) but that it was never likely to get much better. In fact the same point had been made years earlier, for the same reason, by the Israeli linguist Yehoshua Bar-Hillel. The creators of early MT systems were predominantly computer specialists with mathematical expertise, not linguists; what both Bar-Hillel and the ALPAC group argued, in effect, was that these people were naive about the realities of human language. They were too impressed by Warren Weaver's analogy between translation and code-breaking; they did not notice that there is far more to translating from one language to another than the mechanical operations of substitution and rearrangement on which ciphers are based.

MT systems of the 1960s did in fact work in a fashion not too different from an automatic decoding machine: they substituted words for equivalent words listed in an electronic dictionary, shuffled the words round to conform to the target language syntax, and fiddled with the word-endings to get the surface grammar right. What this leaves out is understanding. When a human translates, he continually exploits his understanding of the ideas expressed in the source language in order to decide on the correct equivalent in the target language. This point does not relate specially to high-flown aesthetic considerations: it recurs constantly in the translation of humdrum practical documentation.

Suppose you are translating into French the sentence 'If solvent is found on the platen, the operator should remove it promptly with a clean rag.' The English word 'it' has three possible translations: *l'* if it precedes a word starting with a vowel, *le* or *la* if it precedes a word starting with a consonant and refers to a noun which is respectively masculine or feminine. What does this 'it' refer to – the solvent *(le dissolvant)*, or the platen *(la platine)?* The next word in French will be the translation of 'remove' – this will begin with a vowel if 'it' is the solvent, because to remove a liquid is *enlever* or *essuyer*, but with a consonant if 'it' is the platen, when a verb such as *retirer* would be more appropriate.

A human translator will barely notice the problem: obviously 'it' is the solvent. But what tells him this? Nothing in the language of the English sentence, surely. Rather, we deploy our intelligence and common sense in reasoning, unconsciously, that liquid spilled on a machine part calls for cleaning the part rather than taking it away, and that if one did want to remove a heavy object like a platen, a clean rag would not be much help in doing so. Computers can manipulate symbols mechanically, but they cannot think. Therefore, it seemed, they could never get this sort of decision right; and since this kind of decision is constantly required in translating, Bar-Hillel concluded that what he called 'FAHQT' – fully automatic, high quality translation – would for ever be impossible.

Even if that is true, we understand better than Bar-Hillel did that there is a place for medium-quality translation. But, nowadays, many cognitive scientists would dispute Bar-Hillel's conclusion. Maybe computers can never 'think' – that is more a philosophical than a scientific question; but there exists a flourishing subject called Artificial Intelligence – AI – which is about getting computers to simulate the various types of behaviour that we call intelligent when humans engage in them. AI has made striking advances in a few decades. There exist computer programs which can beat any human player at draughts, and chess programs which give grand masters a run for their money. In the more practical sphere, AI has had considerable success in diagnosing diseases, for instance. Natural language reasoning is a central area of AI research, and many machine translation researchers today would argue that FAHQT is not ruled out in principle: it is just going to take much longer than people imagined back in the 1950s, because the AI software which will enable computers to simulate the reasoning processes by which (for instance) we deduce that 'it' in the example has to refer to solvent rather than platen is far more complex than the substitution and rearrangement routines which take care of the 'codebreaking' aspects of translation.

At present one has to say that the potential contributions of AI techniques to machine translation remain to be established; it is too soon to say with confidence that AI will indeed be able to deliver the hoped-for goods in this area. In a sense, translation is the ultimate challenge for artificial intelligence. Software for playing chess or diagnosing disease has to embody sophisticated routines for simulating one specific area of human knowledge, but with translation it seems that *any* knowledge we have might be just what is needed to solve some particular translation problem. A fully adequate MT system might need to be not just artificially intelligent but artificially omniscient.

Whether or not the hopes of the AI enthusiasts bear fruit, though, it is certainly true that the new wave of MT activity has gained by incorporating a much better understanding than was available in pre-ALPAC days of the nature of human languages as entities with complex structure in their own right. Nowadays it is usual for the backgrounds of MT researchers to involve linguistics as much as, or more than, computing. It is well understood now that *linguistic rules* and *translation software* are independent aspects of an MT system that must be kept rigidly separate.

Anyone with experience of designing complex computer software knows that much hangs on *modularity*. The more one can break down the overall task into separate units which do not need to take account of one another's internal workings, the better the chances of producing a successful system. If a software system is highly modular, a flaw in performance can be localised to one small module and cured. In a non-modular system, changing one small piece of coding inevitably turns out to have unforeseen repercussions elsewhere in the system, and attempts to cure a bug just lead to bigger and bigger messes. A cardinal axiom of modern MT philosophy is that the linguists must be able to change their mind about how best to specify the rules of a source or target language, without this requiring alteration of the software which computer specialists have designed to exploit the language rules in moving from source to target language.

By lucky chance, the changing market for MT systems has had a beneficial effect in making modularity inevitable. While most MT dealt just with the Russian–English language pair, translation systems were normally *direct:* the software converted texts straight from Russian to English, without any identifiable intermediate stages. Imagine trying the direct approach in the case of Eurotra, which involves nine languages: one would need to create 72 entirely independent translation systems, a truly daunting prospect. (Each source language has eight possible target languages: $9 \times 8 = 72$.) Far more economical is to design an indirect system, whereby for each language there is an *analysis* component that converts source texts into a neutral, logical language – an *interlingua* – and a *synthesis* component that converts examples of the interlingua into target language texts. (The interlingua would normally be a purely abstract notation for representing the meanings of texts in a systematic, unambiguous form, rather than a 'language' that anyone actually speaks – though one MT group, at the BSO Company of Utrecht, use Esperanto for their interlingua.) Then translation between all pairings of nine languages needs only nine analysis and nine synthesis components. If the creation of one analysis and one synthesis component together needs effort comparable to the effort needed for a direct system, then the task has been reduced from 72 systems to 9. But actually we have done better still – by enforcing a strict separation between the analysis and synthesis aspects of the translation task we have made it easier to get both aspects right then when the two functions are mingled in a single direct system.

Once analysis and synthesis are clearly distinguished, the really challenging part of designing an MT system is analysis. The fundamental problem of computer translation lies in the fact that almost any element of a source language taken in isolation – whether a word of the vocabulary, a syntactic construction, a verb ending – may correspond to any one of several alternative concepts: human beings are good at using context to decide *which* interpretation to impose on any particular form, and somehow the MT researcher has to get the computer to manage the same trick. Seen from this point of view, perceptions of the nature of different languages change. People usually think of English as an easy language – it has so little grammar. For MT workers, English is the summit of difficulty, for that same reason: it has so few clues showing the machine which interpretation to select. In English it is quite easy to construct a sentence like 'Buck shot cost double last time prices rose', in which every word has at least two grammatically different interpretations: for instance, 'last' is an adjective, but out of context it could equally well be a verb ('to last out') or a noun (a shoemaker's last). This could scarcely happen in any other European language. A leader of the Eurotra project once told me that, after Brussels had got the British using metres and kilogrammes and driving on the right, grammar would have to be next on the list: for MT purposes it was imperative to kit English out with a gender system and a respectable diversity of verb endings. I have wondered ever since whether he was joking...

Modern MT systems normally involve at least the degree of indirectness implied by the interlingua approach. Many systems, Eurotra included, go a stage further still. Rather than using one interlingua, they define a separate logical notation for each language to be translated – thus getting round the problem that some languages involve conceptual distinctions that other languages do not express in any fashion. It would be odd, for instance, for translation from French to German to go through an interlingua which required each verb to be specified as progressive or non-progressive – we need this distinction to make the correct choice in English between *is going* and *goes*, but neither French nor German has it.

Translation now becomes a three-stage process including analysis, *transfer* between source language and target language logical representations, and synthesis. From one point of view this may look like a backward step. Because it uses the transfer approach, Eurotra needs 72 transfer modules in addition to 9 analysis and 9 synthesis modules. But the idea is that transfer between logical representations should involve only those areas where there are genuine conceptual differences between the respective languages, cutting away all the purely superficial differences such as placement of adjectives before the noun in one language and after the noun in another. So each transfer module should be reasonably straightforward to design; and it will deal with real problems of conceptual incompatibility that would have to be addressed separately for individual language-pairs in any fully satisfactory MT system, whether of the transfer, interlingua or direct variety. Meanwhile, the division of the translation process into three parts further adds to modularity, and thus increases the chance of successfully realising sophisticated language-processing ideas in software.

By the 1980s MT was no longer a purely academic enterprise, used in just a few limited situations by government agencies. It was a commercial reality, with systems available off the shelf from profit-making companies and bought by a variety of clients. (Indeed, there developed something of a rift between, on the one hand, AI-oriented academics who chased the rainbow of 'ideal' intelligent translation systems which could become a reality only in the distant future, and on the other hand researchers working in the industrial world who concentrated on producing imperfect but practical systems capable of delivering results here and now.) Here, for comparison with the earlier specimen of 1960s' work, is a sample of translation from German by the system marketed by the Logos Corporation, a transfer-type system dating to about 1983:

> The meaning of/by personal computers as a high-output decentra-
> lized workstation, continuously increases. The claims at the
> printing units are accordingly high, for between 30–45 characters
> must be brought to the paper per second. That asks highest
> quality-standards with regard to stability, color-intensity, resis-
> tance to tearing and durability especially of the printer ribbons.
> Also for the printer of your personal computer, our special-
> cartridges have proved successful characterized.

There is no mistaking the fact that this was translated by a computer. For any purpose more demanding than cursory scanning to locate documents of interest it would require revision, or 'post-editing', by a human translator (and in practice this would normally be done). But the revision could be done quite quickly; this translation is not at all bad.

Let me add, in case I seem to claim too much for current MT, that contemporary systems still can and frequently do fall flat on their faces. French-speaking Eurocrats became so used to seeing the names of their Dutch colleagues – van den Bergh, van Dam, and the like – transformed by Systran into *petit camion* that they petitioned the developers of the system not to eliminate this endearing foible. Or consider another Logos sample, translating a German source text which ran as follows:

> Eine feldweise Steuerung des Auftretens der verschiedenen Felder ist glücklicherweise nicht nötig. Es gibt Gruppen von Feldern, die stets gemeinsam auftreten oder nicht auftreten und die wir deshalb zu sog. 'Feldgruppen' zusammenfassen können.

A good translation would run as follows:

> Monitoring the occurrence of the various fields on a field-by-field basis is fortunately not necessary. There are groups of fields which always occur or fail to occur jointly, and which accordingly we can combine into so-called 'field-groups'.

The form *sog.* is the standard German abbreviation for *sogenannt*, 'so-called'. But the full stop before opening inverted commas and a capital letter looks like the end of a sentence, and *sog* as a complete word does exist in German, the past tense of the verb *saugen*. So Logos fell into the trap, and translated:

> A field-by-field control of the occurrence of the different fields is luckily not necessary. There are groups of fields which occur always commonly, or occur not and which we sucked therefore too...

Even the most obtuse human translator would suspect something amiss; but the computer forges blithely on.

It will be many years, if ever, before MT systems can be guaranteed never to produce howlers like this. But meanwhile the technology has established a clear role for itself. What was once seen as a kind of wizardry by mysterious 'electronic brains' has turned, like so many other computer applications, into a routine part of the workaday world – not at all magical, and far from perfect, but economically quite valuable.

SUGGESTIONS FOR FURTHER READING

As a comprehensive and readable survey of all aspects of MT, W.J. Hutchins, *Machine Translation: Past, Present, Future* (Chichester: Ellis Horwood, 1986) is unrivalled. Margaret King (ed.), *Machine Translation Today: The State of the Art* (Edinburgh University Press, 1987) is rather more technical but contains a number of contributions of general interest.

7   Computer-assisted Language Learning (CALL)

TERRY KALISKI

The ease with which the computer has been accepted as a fundamental part of our everyday existence has been a feature of recent times. Yet at any stage of history, few, if any, technological developments have been welcomed with open arms by all sections of society and 20th-century language teachers are no exception to this rule. The affair between advocates of CALL and the rest of the language teaching profession has yet to come to fruition but there are signs that they may soon begin talking to each other.

There are a number of reasons for the under-utilisation of computers in language teaching. While the young are often computer literate, older members of society express a certain reluctance to embrace the computer and remain unaware of its potential. Similarly, an association in the early days of CALL with behaviourist language learning theory, leading to rote learning and drilling of language items, known to language teachers as 'drill and kill', and this has given CALL a bad image. Language teaching theory has now moved into a 'cognitive', 'communicative' phase, leading some people to take the view that CALL has nothing new to offer. Finally, poorly produced software and a general hobbyist approach which often appears to lack any sense of direction have adversely affected CALL and contributed to a rejection of the medium by many language teachers.

Yet more thoughtful consideration of the question will reveal a number of areas where CALL can be put to good use. These will be looked at later. While much CALL software may still be in the Iron Age in pedagogical terms, there are suggestions of new roles for CALL. Different ways of utilising the computer and reassessing its role, new ideas about programming and technological developments are beginning to open up new possibilities. The computer has a positive role to play in language teaching provided its possibilities and limitations are recognised.

Seymour Papert,[1] writing about computer-aided instruction suggested that in using the computer to teach the child our emphasis was wrong, and the roles should actually be reversed to give the *child* mastery. Papert's observation could equally be applied to language teaching. While the mechanistic image of computer teaching has been dispelled in some areas of teaching there is still a hangover of this attitude in language teaching.

EARLY CALL AND SOME METHODOLOGICAL CONSIDERATIONS

There are a number of acronyms which cover various aspects of computer learning and perhaps we should begin by looking at one or two of these in order to prevent any possible confusion. The more common ones include CAI (computer-aided instruction), which is used mainly in the United States and CAL (computer-assisted learning). From this we get CALL (computer-assisted language learning). While there are a number of other important uses for the computer in the educational field, we will only be looking at CALL here. CAI can be traced back to the late 1950s when American universities adopted the medium for various forms of education including language teaching. In terms of CALL, developments of the 1950s–1960s run parallel with theoretical considerations about language teaching which were dominant at the time. Language teaching was dominated by behaviourist learning theories, a theory of language based on the idea of language as habit, and structuralist linguistic theory emanating from the American structuralist school of linguistics founded by Bloomfield. The method which resulted from this was known as audiolingualism and this was the first method to be based on linguistic and psychological theory.

The basis of the audiolingual (AL) method was that language learning was like building a house – you simply put one brick on top of another. The key to this 'Lego' approach was listening, repetition, remembering and adding to structures which had become habit to the student. One of the principal technological developments associated with AL was the language laboratory, and in some ways the development of computer-based teaching ran parallel to that of the language laboratory. The basic problem here was that at the time these developments were taking place, the behaviourist view of the finite nature of language was being seriously questioned. The consequent changes in teaching methodology which occurred as a result of new ideas on the nature of language led to CALL being

---

[1] S. Papert, *Mindstorms*, Brighton: Harvester Press, 1980.

associated with the stigma of behaviourism and many language teachers viewed CALL in this way.

The fact that CALL was viewed with a certain hostility by language teachers goes beyond mere objections to methodological considerations. Early CALL was designed to be used for self study and most of the input was designed by people other than language teachers, in particular psychologists and the computer industry itself. One of the fears within the teaching profession at the time was that the computer would alter the nature of student/teacher relationships. At Stanford University in the late 1960s, a language teaching program which superseded the teacher was formulated while at New York the teachers working with computers in the language teaching programs were reduced to the role of teaching audiolingual drills.[2] While other programs were less ambitious and saw the role of the computer as an ancillary one, many teachers mistakenly believed that their role would be subverted by the computer.

CALL developments during the 1970s were principally on mainframe systems in universities. For example, one of these which is still in use after various technological modifications, is the PLATO program developed at Illinois University. Developed as a reading and translation course for students studying Russian, the course consisted of three basic components: vocabulary drills, grammar explanations, and drills and translation tests. The addition of touch sensitive screens and audio input to this program has not really altered the basic methodological approach which contains many ideas associated with AL. Methodological changes to a more communicative approach led to a rejection by some teachers of any method associated with behaviourism. It was argued that language with no context, as was the case with many CALL exercises, was of no use and teaching should concentrate on the functional or notional uses of language. Yet it seems clear that certain aspects of the behaviourist method, such as syntactic or vocabulary drilling, are useful weapons in the teacher's armoury and the computer can be a useful ally in this.

The approach to computer learning, particularly in the USA, has been to accent the individualisation of the process. The student is free to proceed at his/her own pace within a strictly controlled situation of programmed learning or instruction. Throughout the 1960s and 1970s, the association of programmed learning and programmed instruction (again a building block approach to learning) with the computer was firmly established. As late as 1981, it was being claimed that computer-assisted learning and programmed learning were essentially the same, and the advent of the microcomputer was merely bringing structuralist

---

[2] G. Holmes and M.E. Kidd. 'Second language learning and computers', *Canadian Modern Language Review*, vol. 38, 1982.

techniques back into the picture. A percentage of contemporary CALL software would support this view but this is not due to the medium but to the poverty of ideas within software programming. More recent developments would suggest that in some areas we are moving away from this position. There is clearly a need to involve those working in the theory and practice of language teaching in the planning and design stages of software if CALL is to develop in a coherent way.

In addition to the CALL mainframe developments already mentioned, there were a number of other projects at other universities and institutions, although it should be remembered that the impact of CALL in relation to the number of institutions was small. The reasons for this were both logistical and financial. Computers were large and the costs of establishing CALL programs was prohibitive. It was not until the advent of the microcomputer in the late 1970s that this position began to change. The microcomputer opened up many possibilities. Firstly, CALL became available to smaller institutions. Secondly, the availability of the hardware meant programming opportunities for those other than professional programmers.

The computer developments which occurred during the late 1970s and early 1980s outstripped the support systems needed to make the computer a worthwhile enterprise for language teaching. Design of software was basically the realm of those interested in programming rather than the result of constructive theoretical consideration. Likewise, piecemeal development of non-standardised hardware has led to incompatibility. While the MS-DOS operating system, as used on IBM PCs and compatibles, is common to many microcomputers, much of the early developmental work in CALL was done on a variety of other machines. CALL programs in Britain were mainly used on the BBC or Spectrum models. The growth in popularity of the larger capacity PCs means that much of CALL software is incompatible with the newer machines, a situation which has been welcomed by many teachers since it wipes the slate clean of much of the dubious software. Since the cost of conversion is high and the markets rather limited, only the most popular of the commercially produced software has been converted.

PRESENT DAY CALL

Many language teaching institutions now utilise computers in various ways. In many schools, computers are used for self study and the students can select the particular CALL program required. Other institutions have computers linked systematically in a local area network (LAN) so that the teacher can control the CALL input with the added bonus of a reduction in software costs. These systems can be linked either to a master PC or to the central system. The advantage of central system networks is that there is access to a greater number of CALL activities. Although some teachers actually use CALL in the classroom, it is probable that the majority of CALL use is by students using it on a self access basis.

At present, most CALL activities fall into three broad categories, although there is an emergent fourth type which is generating interest. Cook identifies these in three general terms.[3] The first of these involves the computer as a kind of 'drill sergeant'. Activities of this type frequently involve the use of uncontextualised language in a way in which the overall goal from a pedagogical viewpoint is unclear. There are a number of software packages which fall into this category including drilling and instructional packages such as 'Grammar Mastery' or 'Screentest for Proficiency' which includes transformation exercises, cloze (gap filling) exercises and other exercises in a fill-in or multiple choice format. The drill sergeant types of program could simply ask the student to provide the correct word or they might provide a substitution drill, such as:

> C. What is on the table? A book?
> S. Yes there is a book on the table.
> C. What is on the table? A pen?
> S. Yes there is a pen on the table.
> etc.

This type of presentation does not appear to be particularly motivating and since a large proportion of CALL involves the use of grammar input there have been various attempts to enliven the process. As Jones and Fortescue point out, there are ways of making these exercises more interesting.[4] This process does not necessarily involve producing joke responses which wear thin on viewing them more than once or using meaningless graphics. The answer is to make the material intrinsically more interesting. For example, it is possible to present comparatives in the 'drill sergeant' manner, or we could use a program such as 'Photofit' in which students draw the features on a graphically presented image. This type of exercise is much more stimulating whether used for self access or as part of a planned lesson and clearly has more communicative potential than the previous example. In Photofit the student is presented with a drawing of a face

---

[3] V.J. Cook. 'Natural language processing as interface between CALL and computing', in W. Mackiewicz (ed.), *Neue Technologien und Fremdsprachen-Ausbildung an den Hochschulen.* Aks Ruhr-Universität Bochum, 1988.

[4] C. Jones and S. Fortescue. *Using Computers in the Language Classroom.* Harlow: Longman, 1987.

and then attempts to reconstruct it from memory by typing in commands such as 'hair' or 'nose'. The computer responds and the student must then decide if the face is the same; if there is a need for adjustment the student can type in comparative adjectives, such as 'bigger' or 'smaller' for the various facial features.

The second type of program, which appears to be the biggest selling and the most popular with students, comes in the 'computer as playmate' category. These are word guessing games which use variations of the conventional cloze techniques or jumbled sentences. The jumbled sentence activity may involve reordering a single sentence or reorganising a piece of text. Thus these exercises can be used for simple syntactic construction or to assist in the development of paragraph organisation. They can be used for self study or to promote discussion if used in a group context. Perhaps the most popular and flexible of these activities is 'Storyboard': a text is displayed and then obliterated, and the student attempts to restore it by guessing the individual words until the original is complete. There are levels of help or 'cheat' options available should the student require them. The student deletes the text and leaves only the title to assist with inferencing. The help feature provides individual letters should the student have problems in guessing the text.

Some software, such as 'Storyboard', has an added advantage in that it can be *authored* by the teacher. This authoring facility means that the textual input can be changed and manipulated according to the wishes of the teacher without the need for any programming knowledge. One of the major problems with earlier programs was that they were complete and could not be altered. Programs which have the authoring facility allow the teacher to make the decisions, rather than rely on a programmer who may have little knowledge of language teaching.

The third type of program is the simulation activity in which the computer acts as adjudicator or oracle. This includes adventure-type scenarios in which the student has to make decisions in order to complete a single mission or those simulations which require decisions to be made on a yearly basis. For example, in 'Great Britain Ltd' students are invited to run the economy of the country based on information given to them by the computer. The students are invited to form a government and then raise taxes based on the needs of areas of government. The computer produces a progress report each year. The process mirrors real-life politics in that, after a five year term, the students usually end up with the economy in total ruin with the computer providing a final analysis. In 'Yellow River Kingdom' (and a number of similar programs) the students are required to make decisions about the numbers of people which need to be assigned to various tasks throughout the year. People have to be assigned to planting the fields, maintaining the dykes and guarding the crops during the three different seasons. The decisions made are vital to the well-being of the village. The dykes have to be maintained to stop the river flooding and guards must be assigned to the fields to stop attacks from robbers. Similarly, there must also be enough people working in the fields. The demand in different areas varies according to the season. If the wrong decisions are made the student (as chief) will be responsible for the resulting deaths.

It is claimed that these games are highly motivating and the decision-making process generates interaction between students. My own observations in this suggest that the motivation may well be shortlived and, as the activity proceeds, the interaction lessens and more arbitrary decisions result. Another problem is the fact that the computer is the sole arbiter in the decision-making process, leaving no room for alternative solutions. Some of the programs are somewhat mathematical in nature, for example 'Great Britain Ltd' or 'Fast Food' (where the student runs a fastfood outlet), and it is difficult to see precisely what the object is, apart from student conversational interaction.

The student assumes a passive role in many CALL activities and while drilling and cloze type exercises have a place in the classroom, modern teaching theory and practice claims to be based on developing interactive language use. Many current CALL programs have no relationship to theories of language and often appear to have been designed merely to demonstrate technological developments rather than contribute to the educational process.

Yet it is clear that the potential role of the computer in language learning goes far beyond the present horse and cart stage: research into what could be termed a fourth role for CALL has been continuing for a number of years. There have been some attempts to relate current language teaching theory to computer activities. If CALL is to become more communicative then there is a need for more interactive material which simulates situations in which real decisions have to be made. Communicative language teaching is based on the need to use language functionally and creates situations, such as booking a hotel, asking directions or applying for a job. To create this in CALL requires changes in the way the computer uses language. One way of doing this is to utilise the ELIZA techniques, developed by Weizenbaum in the 1960s. This type of program operates by looking for keywords and constructing a conversation around them. The effect is quite successful in that the computer appears to reply to the typed input in an intelligent way. For example, if the student types 'Could I have a ticket to London please?' the computer may respond with 'single or return?' or some other option. There are then a number of programmed responses which create the illusion of conversational interaction. Whereas many computer programs had preset dialogues, the responses of ELIZA programs can vary considerably and produce many different conversations.

A program named 'Escape from Utopia' is an adventure scenario during which the students must remain undetected in Utopia while on a secret mission.[5] This game attempts to utilise the techniques used in the classroom in that it creates dialogues and simulations, and by providing a map which the student must use to reach a destination, it also uses what is known as information gap exercises. While this can be done at a superficial level there are a number of problems if one is to produce more sophisticated 'conversation'. Clearly, programming for the possibilities of conversational options presents major problems given the wide number of possible responses to any particular situation. ELIZA matches strings of letters rather than syntactically parsing the input. As such it may produce strange responses to particular items. One of the ways of avoiding this is to make use of natural language parsing programs (see chapter 4).

In an attempt to break what Johns described as the 'glorified quizmaster' role of the computer, research has been continuing on a number of CALL strategies and the role the computer can assume. The computer can operate in a more generative way and is capable of being used to explain grammatical structures and to generate these structures and utilise these features in a more interactive way. The computer is given a rule system rather than a limited amount of data and from these rules the computer analyses the input. For example, a set of spelling rules in English can be used to analyse word endings and from this the student could then infer the rule for a particular case, a process which would appear to be not dissimilar to the way the learner actually appears to develop knowledge of a second language rule system. Similarly, natural language processing or syntactic parsing techniques can also be used to show the student the structure of the target language.

The 'exploratory CALL' approach suggests a role reversal for the computer in which the machine is viewed not as the oracle but as a pedagogue which is available if required or as a 'dumb machine' which the students can pit their wits against.[6] The object is for students to test the effectiveness of a program by working out how it is done or by attempting to prove the machine wrong, thus making the program part of the learning process in that hypotheses about aspects of language are being tested.

CALL and the language teacher

Although much of CALL software is somewhat limited, the computer has a number of areas in which it can be a useful teaching aid. The teacher who merely

---

[5] Written by Vivian Cook in 1984.
[6] J. Higgins. 'Smart learners and dumb machines', *System*, vol. 14, no. 2, 1986.

places students in front of a machine and tells them to get on with it is unlikely to achieve very much, but if the computer is integrated into classroom activities in a specific way there may well be positive advantages. Certain types of learner are motivated by using the computer, particularly the younger learners; using the computer may well help to alleviate the boredom which is often caused by different learning speeds within particular language groups. Many CALL activities operate on a competitive basis with systems for measuring the results, and learners often appear to be motivated by the element of competition.

Much of the work of the teacher in the early stage of language development involves the teaching of essential structures and the computer seems suited to this task, particularly if the programs can be authored to suit particular needs. Learner development is an uneven process and time is often spent on what, for some students, is unnecessary repetition. Students working at their own pace can resolve some of these problems. This could enable the teacher to spend more time with individuals. Many CALL programs also provide instant feedback, which is a positive incentive to the student.

Word-processing provides another area for CALL. Students often have trouble with writing and the finished result can be somewhat demotivating if it is full of assorted mistakes and crossings out. Using the word-processor can solve this problem while at the same time helping to develop various skills, like putting a text together or correcting their own errors. The student is also learning a useful skill which again can be motivating in itself.

Other uses for the computer include being used as an electronic blackboard able to handle a wide variety of information which can be modified by the teacher. Databases can also be utilised for the storing of information and progress of individual students. Routine marking and checking work can also be handled by the computer and there are some commercially produced tests on the market which can ease the task of the teacher. Style checkers which examine students' written work for grammatical errors and provide explanations for mistakes are available, and programs capable of semantic processing will add to this capability in the future. The teacher can also point out to students their individual weaknesses and the student can then proceed to work on these without embarrassment until an individual target is achieved. CALL programs do not have 'off days' and the relationship with the student is different in that there are no personality factors or status relationships involved. CALL can also be a source of the comprehensible input considered to be necessary for the language acquisition process.

Despite these advantages, there are a number of problems associated with using CALL. One of the frequent criticisms concerns the fact that there is no spoken contact between the student and the computer and this fundamentally alters the nature of interaction. While there are systems which use speech, this is in the form of operating a tape recorder with prerecorded speech through a computer interface or in conjunction with a particular CALL program. It will be several years before good-quality synthesised speech becomes available, and there will be many problems in developing its use. The more sophisticated tape systems are not cheap, while those which are not wholly controlled by the computer have certain problems with retrieval. The nature of human conversation is divergent and unpredictable, and most of us have a number of strategies and our experience of the world to draw upon when we make a response. No machine can do this, and many CALL programs will refuse to accept logical alternatives offered by the student, accepting only the programmed input. Similarly, teachers have a variety of strategies at their disposal while CALL programs frequently operate within rigid paradigms.

The question of evaluating precisely what happens during a CALL session also presents problems. While the pedagogical aspects of the software can be evaluated, we simply do not know enough about the language acquisition process to make any realistic judgements. Teaching methodology expresses the need for communicative interaction both to foster conscious learning and to facilitate the acquisition process. One of the arguments against CALL is that it focuses on the conscious side of learning, which could be equated with linguistic accuracy, rather than, in line with current theory, the development of linguistic fluency. While some have advocated that the computer is flexible enough to serve a variety of learning theories, there is not enough evidence to reach a conclusion either way. While it may be true that anyone learning a language should be exposed to as much language as possible, it may be that much of the language offered by CALL is not the optimum kind of input.

Perhaps the major problem with CALL at the moment is the absence of any clear methodology or models which express the role of what may potentially be a powerful teaching aid. At present, it is not quite clear what the relationship between activity type and learning style really is. There is a need for linguistic description which can account for language teaching points which are embedded in CALL materials. Phillips lists a number of areas in which the role of CALL must be more clearly defined.[7] These include defining the role of the teacher within CALL, relating the materials to current theory and defining the purpose of the CALL materials. Clear methodological consideration has been given to other teaching aids in the classroom, such as the use of video and cassette

---

[7] M. Phillips. 'Language learning and information technology', *System* vol. 13, no. 2, 1985.

recorders and the teacher perceives these as useful allies, whereas the computer is still sometimes regarded with suspicion.

CALL IN THE FUTURE

At the present time CALL is in a transitional stage, where the wave of novelty and innovation has passed; but despite the uncertainties which surround its future, there is a future in language teaching for CALL if the potential is harnessed correctly. In reality, much of CALL is still at the horse and cart stage, although there have been a number of promising developments. One of the research areas for CALL has been in 'intelligent CALL'. This approach is not new: artificial intelligence programs, such as Winograd's SHRDLU from the 1960s, have shown that computers can respond in an interactive way in a limited semantic field. The object of this is to offer a genuine analytical approach to language rather than a synthetic one. Many CALL programs consist of totally uncontextualised language which bears no relation to the reality of human language interaction. Intelligent CALL attempts to remedy this by generating language rather than just analysing textual input and producing a preprogrammed response. If we consider the number of linguistic rules we unconsciously acquire, or our ability to recognise ambiguity in language, then some of the problems of programming intelligent CALL become clear. Most of the programs in this area operate within a restricted semantic field due to the difficulties of constructing semantic rule systems. Lexical storage and syntactic rules present fewer problems. Thus, it seems likely that intelligent CALL will operate within a restricted semantic world for some time to come.

As the microcomputer becomes more powerful, the potential for use in various areas expands. One area of interest for both language teacher and student is sentence concordance and collocations, using techniques such as those described in chapter 2: collocations are a huge part of the native speaker's armoury and knowing which words are habitually associated with which and when to use a particular phrase presents problems for the language learner. Like phrasal verbs and idioms, these collocations have to be remembered and CALL programs could be useful here.

There are also several developments in the linking of different technologies. At present most of the visual presentation of information in the classroom is in the form of videotape but developments in videodisc technology have produced a superior product which, when linked to a computer, offer faster retrieval and more interactive potential than videotape. The only problem at the moment is the cost. NEWSIM is another idea which links technologies.[8] A short-wave radio is linked by an interface to a microcomputer and printer and taps into the radio transmissions of various sources, such as press agencies, to obtain unedited news which can then be exploited in a number of ways. Textbooks and other produced materials, even if authentic, quickly become stale and NEWSIM provides an answer to this problem.

Another potential use for the computer is in pronunciation teaching. While it is possible to get a computer to produce synthetic speech, it is not yet a practical proposition for the language teacher. However, spectrographic representations of words and phonemes could provide a useful way for the student to practise pronunciation, and programs have been developed in which sounds produced by the teacher are analysed and displayed and the student has to attempt to get a similar pattern on the screen. One of the benefits of this is that the student gets instant feedback. The potential for this type of program in many areas of pronunciation, including stress and intonation, make this an interesting area for development.

The overall trend in CALL is that programs are becoming more and more generative in nature. The interaction will be governed much more by the needs of the student, and programs which meet those needs and demands will replace many of those which were written for a particular purpose. This is not to deny the usefulness of drilling programs in language teaching, but there is a need for more interaction which equates with current language teaching theory.

In this short review, I have looked at various aspects of CALL, past, present and future. Quite what the future actually will be for CALL is not certain. One could take the pessimistic view held by many teachers that CALL does nothing that any language teacher could not do better, and therefore predict that there is no future for the computer in language learning. One could equally take the view that, as the technology develops, more efficient ways of exploiting it will make it a valuable teaching aid.

SUGGESTIONS FOR FURTHER READING

There are some excellent books which deal with various aspects of CALL. For those interested in the overall perspective, I would recommend K. Ahmad, G. Corbett, M. Rogers, and R. Sussex *Computers, Language Learning and Language Teaching* (Cambridge University Press, 1985), or J. Higgins and T. Johns

---

[8] D.Crookall. 'Media gaming and NEWSIM – a computer-assisted real news simulation', *System*, vol. 13, no. 3, 1985.

Computers in Language Learning (London: Collins, 1984). C. Jones and S. Fortescue *Using Computers in the Language Classroom* (Harlow: Longman, 1987), is aimed at teachers and provides illustration and description of contemporary teaching software. D. Hardisty, and S. Windeatt *C.A.L.L.* (Oxford University Press, 1989) offers the language teacher numerous ways of exploiting CALL materials, while those who wish to understand some of the basic programming involved may find M. Kenning and M-M. Kenning *An Introduction to Computer Assisted Language Learning* (Oxford University Press, 1983) a good place to start. A more recent alternative is G. Davies *Talking BASIC* (London: Cassell, 1985).

INDEX